ENGLISH SONNETS

ENGLISH SONNETS

edited with an introduction by
WALT TAYLOR

LONGMANS, GREEN AND CO.
LONDON · NEW YORK · TORONTO

LONGMANS, GREEN AND CO. LTD.
OF PATERNOSTER ROW

43 ALBERT DRIVE, LONDON, S.W. 19
NICOL ROAD, BOMBAY
17 CHITTARANJAN AVENUE, CALCUTTA
36A MOUNT ROAD, MADRAS

LONGMANS, GREEN AND CO.
55 FIFTH AVENUE, NEW YORK 3

LONGMANS, GREEN AND CO.
215 VICTORIA STREET, TORONTO I

First published 1947

CODE NUMBER 18251

PRINTED IN GREAT BRITAIN BY ROBERT MACLEHOSE AND CO. LTD.
AT THE UNIVERSITY PRESS, GLASGOW

INTRODUCTION

No satisfactory definition of a sonnet has yet been made because critics have been trying to say what a sonnet ought to be instead of trying to say what a sonnet actually is. The variety of length and of pattern makes a rigid definition of the English sonnet form impossible; and the variety of subject shows that the matter, or 'inspiration', of the poem may be anything whatsoever. Most of them are written in fourteen lines; and nearly all of them are rhymed—to limit the definition of the form more closely than that would be to exclude some of our greatest sonnets.

There are also poems of genuine poetical value written in fourteen lines with a conventional sonnet rhyme-scheme which are not sonnets; for example James Stephens' *Seumas Beg* is not a sonnet:

> *A man was sitting underneath a tree*
> *Outside a village, and he asked me what*
> *Name was upon this place, and said that he*
> *Was never here before. He told a lot*
> *Of stories to me too. His nose was flat.*
> *I asked him how it happened, and he said*
> *The first mate of the Mary Anne done that*
> *With a marling spike one day, but he was dead,*
> *And jolly good job too; and he'd have gone*
> *A long way to have killed him, and he had*
> *A gold ring in one ear; the other one*
> *'Was bit off by a crocodile, bedad.'*
> *That's what he said. He taught me how to chew.*
> *He was a real nice man. He liked me too.*

A sonnet is not a narrative poem; though a vague thread of narrative, shown chiefly by the change of mood of the sonneteer, can link together a sonnet-sequence.

An attempt has been made by some critics to apply the word 'sonnet' in English to only one kind of sonnet, the so-called 'Italian' or 'Petrarchan' form, a poem of fourteen ten-syllable iambic lines rhyming *abba, abba, cde, cde,* and divided or divisible into an octave followed by a sestet, or an octave followed by two tercets. The Italians themselves had several forms of the sonnet; and that this one 'Italian' form should be taken as the sole legitimate English form is absurd. Yet those critics have seriously (all the more seriously because narrowmindedly) condemned the sonnets of Shakespeare and of Milton, because they did not conform to the critics' idea of a sonnet.

Other critics would accept both this 'Italian' form and the so-called 'English' or 'Shakespearean' form, again a poem of fourteen ten-syllable iambic lines, but rhyming *abab, cdcd, efef, gg,* and divided or divisible into three quatrains followed by a couplet. A glance through this book will show that many other rhyme-schemes are possible. An effort to tabulate them all would be hopeless.

Wilfrid Scawen Blunt attempted sonnets in assonance instead of rhyme; and other poets since his time have done the same: a successful sonnet in assonance has been written by John Lehmann:

> *To penetrate that room is my desire,*
> *The extreme attic of the mind, that lies*
> *Just beyond the last bend in the corridor.*
> *Writing I do it. Phrases, poems are keys.*
> *Loving's another way (but not so sure).*
> *A fire's in there, I think, there's truth at last*
> *Deep in a lumber chest. Sometimes I'm near,*
> *But draughts put out the matches, and I'm lost.*
> *Sometimes I'm lucky, find a key to turn,*
> *Open an inch or two,—but always then*
> *A bell rings, someone calls, or cries of 'fire'*

Arrest my hand when nothing's known or seen,
And running down the stairs again I mourn.

—which happens to be in thirteen lines. John Freeman
attempted a rhymeless sonnet, entitled *Rhymeless*, which he
spoilt by ending it with a couplet: a perfect rhymeless, i.e.
blank verse, sonnet is Lascelles Abercrombie's *Epitaph*,
included in this anthology. A modern poet could find a
good precedent to justify any number of lines from twelve
to sixteen (and Hopkins has produced a beautiful form
which he called the Curtal-sonnet, in ten and a half lines—
see his *Pied Beauty* on p. 159), and any rhyme-scheme or
lack of rhyme. To mention only two of the greatest sonneteers, Shakespeare could be quoted as having written a sonnet in couplets, or a sonnet in twelve lines; and Milton could
be quoted as having made no break in the movement of a
sonnet after the eighth line.

English sonnets vary still more in subject than they do in
form. In Italy the sonnet had been used chiefly for love-
poems, moralisations on death, for private letters, and
personal invective. In England it was used first as a love-
poem—the sonnets of Wyatt and the Earl of Surrey were
first made public in 1557 in the volume of *Songs and Sonnets*
edited by Richard Tottel, known usually as Tottel's
Miscellany. Then, as there is such a close association of love
with death in the English mind, sonnets were also written
on death, and sleep, and the passage of time; and elegies
were written in this form on the death of personal friends.
But already in Elizabethan times, when there was a fashion
for everyone to write sonnets—quite a craze for them in
the fifteen nineties, comparable to the crossword craze of
the nineteen thirties—the sonnet was used for a large
variety of other purposes: humour will always appear in
any English literary form, and religious devotion, and love
of nature, and the passion for personal and political liberty,

and admiration for honesty. Even the English weather has inspired sonnets—joyful and melancholy. All the chief themes of English literature are treated in sonnets—even literary criticism, including criticism of the sonnet form itself. The only 'trick' sonnet admitted into this collection is that of Edgar Allen Poe. Perhaps the following amusing sonnet by Lamb might have been included; for though it is not great poetry it is the perfect album verse:

In the Album of Mrs. Jane Towers

Lady unknown, who crav'st from me Unknown
The trifle of a verse these leaves to grace,
How shall I find fit matter? with what face
Address a face that ne'er to me was shown?
Thy looks, tones, gestures, manners, and what not,
Conjecturing, I wander in the dark.
I know thee only Sister to Charles Clarke!
But at thy name my cold Muse waxes hot,
And swears that thou art such a one as he,
Warm, laughter-loving, with a touch of madness,
Wild, glee-provoking, pouring oil of gladness
From frank heart without guile. And, if thou be
The pure reverse of this, and I mistake—
Demure one, I will like thee for his sake.

Recently some poets have used the sonnet form for objective description of nature, but particularly of animals, witness Roy Campbell's *Zebras* (p. 182), and Yvonne ffrench's *Daybreak in the Tropics*:

Grey as the banks of mud on which they tilt
Their armoured heads, the alligators smile
Alternately disclosing greed and guile,
While staring at the thickly-moving silt.

And when the suffocating night has gone
Discovered by the dawn in quick surprise,
They blink the shutters of their gilded eyes
And turn and plunge into the Amazon.

Feeling the sun's incendiary hand
Ignite the densely vegetated land
Parrots and brilliant parrakeets emerge;
And leaving their green palaces and domes
They scream across the forest's leafy verge
Like fugitives forsaking stricken homes.

Such 'sonnets' are apt to be simple fourteen-lined nature poems: they are more satisfying when a certain thought or reflection is expressed or implied, as it is in Terence Tiller's *Aquarium*:

Shut in their soundless waves, the fish
turn upwards, nibbling air; or swim
with looping bodies to the dim
caressing glass, a green wish.
The watcher taps: unheeding him
they hang like blunted darts; and swerve
with flat fan-motions, in a curve
easy as water, to the brim.

Are they alive there, in that world
so rippled, channelled, starred, cold-curled,
alien, but three-dimensional?

Our wishes do not light their eyes;
they are content, and will not rise
or heed the tapping on the wall.

—which happens to be in lines of eight syllables, a form which could be justified, if justification were thought necessary, by reference back to John Lyly.

It is the mood of the poet which makes him write in the sonnet form—not his subject, or his way of treating his subject. Certain moods of contemplation, or of deep feeling—usually passing moods—can be perfectly expressed, in fact demand expression, in this brief but closely woven form.

The sonnets in this anthology have been chosen not on a counting of lines and an arrangement of rhymes, but on literary merit. The question asked was, Is this a first-rate sonnet of its kind? The result has been the inclusion of some writers who had become wellnigh forgotten, and the omission of many writers who were thought to be good sonneteers by their contemporaries, particularly in the last century; for there has been no attempt to represent authors by their best work if that work was not of the highest standard. That criterion (which could well be applied by all anthologists of poetry) was especially necessary to a sonnet anthology both because thousands of Englishmen have written sonnets and because our literature is rich in sonnets of the very first quality.

As part of his duty not to tamper with the text, or the spelling, or the punctuation, of his authors more than need be, the editor has avoided the impertinence of adding a title to those sonnets which in the opinion of the author needed none. He wishes to repeat the curse of Chaucer on all bad editors—

> *Under thy lokkes thou most have the scalle,*
> *But after my making thou wryte trewe*

—hoping himself to escape the curse.

ACKNOWLEDGMENTS

My thanks are due to the publishers for enabling me to use copyright material, for which I am indebted to the following:

Messrs. Martin Secker & Warburg Ltd. for *The Fear* and *Epitaph* by Lascelles Abercrombie; Mr. Edmund Blunden for *The Poor Man's Pig*; the author's executors and Messrs. Macmillan & Co. Ltd. for *Esther, Honour Dishonoured* and *Depreciating her Beauty* from *The Poetical Works of Wilfrid Scawen Blunt*; the Clarendon Press, Oxford, for *The Work is Done, The fabled sea-snake, My Lady pleases me,* and *I care not if I live* from *The Growth of Love* by Robert Bridges (*Poetical Works*); the author's representatives and Messrs. Sidgwick & Jackson Ltd. for *Waikiki, O Death will find me, long before I tire, The Dead I, The Dead II, Failure, The Hill, The Soldier, Clouds,* and *Not with vain tears, when we're beyond the sun* from *The Collected Poems of Rupert Brooke*; Messrs. Jonathan Cape Ltd. for *The Life After Death* from *The Notebooks of Samuel Butler* edited by Henry Festing Jones; Mr. Roy Campbell and Messrs. Faber & Faber Ltd. for *The Zebras* and *The Serf*; Messrs. Martin Secker & Warburg Ltd. for *Forgetfulness* by Lord Alfred Douglas; the author's representatives and Messrs. Sidgwick & Jackson Ltd. for *We have laid up simples against forgetfulness* from *The Poems of John Drinkwater*; Miss Yvonne ffrench for *Daybreak in the Tropics*; Mrs. Ayrton Gould, J.P., for *This is the horror that, night after night* by Gerald Gould; the Trustees of the Estate of Thomas Hardy, and Messrs. Macmillan & Co. Ltd. for *Hap, She to Him* and *To a Lady* from *The Collected Poems of Thomas Hardy*; the poet's family and the Oxford University Press for *Pied Beauty, Hurrahing in Harvest, Felix Randal, No worst, there is none, The Sea and the Skylark, The Windhover,* and *Thou art indeed just, Lord, if I contend* from *The Poems of Gerard Manley Hopkins*; Messrs. George Allen & Unwin for the poem entitled *Bagley Wood* beginning *The night is full of stars* from *The Collected Poems* of Lionel Johnson; the representatives of the late Andrew Lang for *The Odyssey* and *Herodotus in Egypt,* from *The Poetical Works of Andrew Lang* published by Longmans Green & Co. Ltd.; Mr. John Lehmann for *To penetrate that room is my desire*; the Society of Authors, Dr. Masefield, O.M., and the Macmillan Company of New York for *Here in the self is all that man can know,* and *Let that which is to come be as it may,* from *Collected Poems* published by Wm. Heinemann Ltd.; the Trustees of the Estate of George Meredith, and Messrs. Constable & Co. Ltd. for *We saw the swallows gathering in the sky, Lucifer in Starlight,* and *Earth's Secret*; the author's representatives and Messrs. Macmillan & Co. Ltd. for *Would God it were morning* from the *Collected Poems of F. W. H. Myers*; the author's representatives and Messrs Chatto & Windus for *Anthem for Doomed Youth* by Wilfred Owen; the author and the Hogarth Press for *Dragon Fly Love* by Mr. William Plomer from *Family Tree*; Mr. Siegfried Sassoon for *Dreamers, The Glory of Women, Strangeness of Heart* and *On Passing the New Menin Gate*; Messrs. Macmillan & Co. Ltd. for *Seumas Beg* by James Stephens; Messrs. Burns Oates & Washbourne Ltd. for *Ad Amicam* by Francis Thompson; Mr. Terence Tiller for *Aquarium*; Lady Maureen Watson for *In City Pent* by Sir William Watson; Mr. Vyvyan Holland for *Written in Holy Week at Genoa, Santa Decca, To Liberty,* and *Impressions de Voyage* by Oscar Wilde; Messrs. Ernest Benn Ltd. for *Prolegomena to any Future Satire* by Humbert Wolfe; Mrs. W. B. Yeats for *The Folly of Being Comforted* and *The Fascination of What's Difficult* from *The Collected Poems of W. B. Yeats* published by Macmillan & Co. Ltd.

CONTENTS

xiii

CONTENTS

CONTENTS

XV

CONTENTS

Farewell, Love, and all thy laws for ever!
Thy baited hooks shall tangle me no more:
Senec and Plato call me from thy lore
To perfect wealth my wit to endeavour.
In blind errour when that I did persèver,
Thy sharp repulse, that pricketh aye so sore,
Taught me in trifles that I set no store;
But 'scape forththence, since liberty is liever.
Therefore, farewell! go trouble younger hearts,
And in me claim no more authority:
With idle youth go use thy property,
And thereon spend thy many brittle darts;
    For hitherto though I have lost my time,
    Me list no longer rotten boughs to climb.

The lover having dreamed enjoying of his love,
complaineth that the dream is not either
longer or truer

Unstable dream, according to the place,
Be steadfast once, or else at least be true:
By tasted sweetness make me not to rue
The sudden loss of thy false feignèd grace.
By good respect, in such a dangerous case,
Thou brought'st not her into these tossing seas;
But mad'st my sprite to live, my care to increase,
My body in tempest her delight to embrace.
The body dead, the sprite had his desire;
Painless was the one, the other in delight.
Why then, alas, did it not keep it right,
But thus return to leap into the fire;
    And when it was at wish, could not remain?
    Such mocks of dreams do turn to deadly pain.

wealth: joy, weal.   liever: preferable.

Whoso list to hunt, I know where is an hind,
But as for me, alas! I may no more.
The vain travail hath wearied me so sore,
I am of them that furthest come behind.
Yet may I by no means my wearied mind
Draw from the deer; but as she fleeth afore
Fainting I follow. I leave off therefore,
Since in a net I seek to hold the wind.
Who list her hunt, I put him out of doubt,
As well as I, may spend his time in vain;
And graven with diamonds in letters plain
There is written, her fair neck round about,
    '*Noli me tangere*, for Caesar's I am,
    And wild for to hold, though I seem tame.'

Ye that in love find luck and sweet abundance,
And live in lust of joyful jollity,
Arise for shame, do 'way your sluggardy:
Arise I say, do May some observance:
Let me in bed lie, dreaming of mischance.
Let me remember my mishaps unhappy
That me betide in May most commonly:
As one whom love list little to advance.
Stephen said true, that my nativity
Mischancèd was with the ruler of May.
He guessed, I prove, of that the verity.
In May my wealth, and eke my wits, I say,
Have stood so oft in such perplexity.
Joy, let me dream of your felicity.

Stephen: the person (otherwise unknown) who cast the author's horo-
scope.

2

My galley, chargèd with forgetfulness,
Thorough sharp seas in winter nights doth pass
'Tween rock and rock; and eke my foe, alas,
That is my lord, steereth with cruelness;
And every oar a thought in readiness
As though that death were light in such a case.
An endless wind doth tear the sail apace
Of forcèd sighs, and trusty fearfulness.
A rain of tears, a cloud of dark disdain,
Have done the wearied cords great hinderance,
Wreathèd with error and with ignorance.
The stars be hid that led me to this pain.
Drownèd in reason, that should me comfort,
And I remain despairing of the port.

Divers do use, as I have heard and know,
When that to change their ladies do begin,
To moan and wail and never for to lynn;
Hoping thereby to 'pease their painful woe.
And some there be that, when it chanceth so
That women change and hate where love hath been,
They call them false and think with words to win
The hearts of them which otherwhere do grow.
But as for me, though that by chance indeed
Change hath outworn the favour that I had,
I will not wail, lament, nor yet be sad,
Nor call her false that falsely did me feed;
But let it pass and think it is of kind
That often change doth please a woman's mind.

lynn: cease.   feed: *sc.* with hope.   of kind: by nature.

3

HENRY HOWARD, EARL OF SURREY

Description of Spring
Wherein each thing renews, save only the lover

The soote season, that bud and bloom forth brings,
With green hath clad the hill, and eke the vale.
The nightingale with feathers new she sings;
The turtle to her mate hath told her tale.
Summer is come, for every spray now springs,
The hart hath hung his old head on the pale;
The buck in brake his winter coat he flings;
The fishes flete with new repaired scale;
The adder all her slough away she slings;
The swift swallow pursueth the fliës smale;
The busy bee her honey now she mings;
Winter is worn that was the flowers' bale.
    And thus I see among these pleasant things
    Each care decays, and yet my sorrow springs!

Set me where as the sun doth parch the green,
Or where his beams do not dissolve the ice;
In temperate heat, where he is felt and seen;
In presence pressed of people mad, or wise;
Set me in high, or yet in low degree;
In longest night, or in the shortest day;
In clearest sky, or where clouds thickest be;
In lusty youth, or when my hairs are gray;
Set me in heaven, in earth, or else in hell;
In hill or dale, or in the foaming flood;
Thrall, or at large, alive whereso I dwell;
Sick, or in health; in evil fame, or good:
    Hers will I be! and only with this thought
    Content myself; although my chance be nought!

soote: sweet   flete: flit, hasten.   mings: mixes.

4

A Complaint by Night of the Lover not beloved

Alas! so all things now do hold their peace!
Heaven and earth disturbèd in no thing;
The beasts, the air, the birds their song do cease;
The nightès car the stars about doth bring.
Calm is the sea; the waves work less and less:
So am not I, whom love, alas! doth wring,
Bringing before my face the great increase
Of my desires, whereat I weep and sing,
In joy and woe, as in a doubtful ease.
For my sweet thoughts sometime do pleasure bring;
But by and by, the cause of my disease
Gives me a pang, that inwardly doth sting.
    When that I think what grief it is again,
    To live and lack the thing should rid my pain.

I never saw you, madam, lay apart
Your cornet black, in cold nor yet in heat,
Sith first ye knew of my desire so great,
Which other fancies chased clean from my heart.
Whiles to myself I did the thought reserve,
That so unware did wound my woeful breast,
Pity I saw within your heart did rest.
But since ye knew I did you love and serve,
Your golden tress was clad alway in black,
Your smiling looks were hid thus evermore,
All that withdrawn that I did crave so sore.
So doth this cornet govern me, alack!
    In summer's sun, in winter breath of frost,
    Of your fair eyes whereby the light is lost.

Cornet: a head-dress such as is still worn by Sisters of Charity, hiding the
hair and shading the face.

The Shepherd's Conceit of Prometheus

Prometheus, when first from heaven high
He brought down fire, ere then on earth unseen,
Fond of the light, a satyr, standing by,
Gave it a kiss, as it like sweet had been.
Feeling forthwith the other's burning power,
Wood with the smart, with shouts and shriekings shrill,
He sought his ease in river, field and bower,
But for the time his grief went with him still.
So silly I, with that unwonted sight,
In human shape an angel from above,
Feeding mine eyes, the impression there did light,
That since I run and rest as pleaseth Love.
  The difference is, the satyr's lips, my heart,—
  He for a while, I evermore have smart.

EDMUND SPENSER

New year, forth looking out of Janus' gate,
  doth seem to promise hope of new delight;
  and bidding th' old Adieu, his passèd date
  bids all old thoughts to die in dumpish sprite:
And calling forth out of sad winter's night
  fresh Love that long hath slept in cheerless bower,
  wills him awake, and soon about him dight
  his wanton wings and darts of deadly power.
For lusty Spring now in his timely hour
  is ready to come forth him to receive,
  and warns the earth with divers-coloured flower
  to deck herself, and her fair mantle weave.
Then you, fair flower, in whom fresh youth doth reign,
  prepare yourself new love to entertain.

Wood: mad.

6

Rudely thou wrongest my dear heart's desire,
    in finding fault with her too portly pride:
    the thing which I do most in her admire
    is of the world unworthy most envied.
For in those lofty looks is close implied
    scorn of base things, and 'sdain of foul dishonour,
    threatening rash eyes which gaze on her so wide
    that loosely they ne dare to look upon her.
Such pride is praise, such portliness is honour,
    that boldened innocence bears in her eyes;
    and her fair countenance like a goodly banner
    spreads in defiance of all enemies.
Was never in this world aught worthy tried
    without some spark of such self-pleasing pride.

Be nought dismayed that her unmovèd mind
    doth still persist in her rebellious pride:
    such love not like to lusts of baser kind,
    the harder won, the firmer will abide.
The dureful oak, whose sap is not yet dried,
    is long ere it conceive the kindling fire;
    but, when it once doth burn, it doth divide
    great heat, and makes his flames to heaven aspire.
So hard it is to kindle new desire
    in gentle breast, that shall endure for ever:
    deep is the wound that dints the parts entire
    with chaste affects that naught but death can sever.
Then think not long in taking little pain
    to knit the knot that ever shall remain.

Unrighteous lord of love, what law is this,
    that me thou makest thus tormented be,
    the whiles she lordeth in licentious bliss
    of her free will, scorning both thee and me?
See how the tyraness doth joy to see
    the huge massàcres which her eyes do make,
    and humbled hearts brings captive unto thee,
    that thou of them mayst mighty vengeance take.
But her proud heart do thou a little shake,
    and that high look with which she doth control
    all this world's pride bow to a baser make,
    and all her faults in thy black book enrol:
That I may laugh at her in equal sort
    as she doth laugh at me, and makes my pain her sport.

In that proud port, which her so goodly graceth,
    whiles her fair face she rears up to the sky,
    and to the ground her eyelids low embaseth,
    most goodly temperature ye may descry,
Mild humbless mixt with awful majesty.
    For, looking on the earth whence she was born,
    her mind remembereth her mortality;
    whatso is fairest shall to earth return.
But that same lofty countenance seems to scorn
    base thing, and think how she to heaven may climb;
    treading down earth as loathsome and forlorn,
    that hinders heavenly thoughts with drossy slime.
Yet lowly still vouchsafe to look on me;
    such lowliness shall make you lofty be.

The glorious portrait of that Angel's face,
    made to amaze weak men's confusèd skill,
    and this world's worthless glory to embase,
    what pen, what pencil, can express her fill?
For though he colours could devise at will,
    and eke his learned hand at pleasure guide,
    lest, trembling, it his workmanship should spill,
    yet many wondrous things there are beside.
The sweet eye-glances, that like arrows glide,
    the charming smiles, that rob sense from the heart,
    the lovely pleasance, and the lofty pride,
    cannot expressèd be by any art.
A greater craftsman's hand thereto doth need,
    that can express the life of things indeed.

The merry Cuckoo, messenger of Spring,
    his trumpet shrill hath thrice already sounded,
    that warns all lovers wait upon their king,
    who now is coming forth with garland crownèd.
With noise whereof the choir of birds resounded
    their anthems sweet devisèd of love's praise,
    that all the woods their echoes back rebounded,
    as if they knew the meaning of their lays.
But mongst them all which did love's honour raise,
    no word was heard of her that most it ought;
    but she his precept proudly disobeys,
    and doth his idle message set at nought.
Therefore, O Love, unless she turn to thee
    ere Cuckoo end, let her a rebel be.

Was it the work of nature or of art
  which tempered so the feature of her face,
    that pride and meekness mixt by equal part
    do both appear to adorn her beauty's grace?
For with mild pleasance, which doth pride displace,
    she to her love doth lookers' eyes allure;
    and with stern countenance back again doth chase
    their looser looks that stir up lusts impure.
With such strange terms her eyes she doth inure,
    that with one look she doth my life dismay,
    and with another doth it straight recure;
    her smile me draws, her frown me drives away.
Thus doth she train and teach me with her looks:
    such art of eyes I never read in books.

This holy season, fit to fast and pray,
    men to devotion ought to be inclined;
    therefore I likewise on so holy day
    for my sweet Saint some service fit will find.
Her temple fair is built within my mind,
    in which her glorious image placèd is,
    on which my thoughts do day and night attend
    like sacred priests that never think amiss.
There I to her as th'author of my bliss
    will build an altar to appease her ire,
    and on the same my heart will sacrifice,
    burning in flames of pure and chaste desire;
The which vouchsafe O godess to accept,
    amongst thy dearest relics to be kept.

Sweet is the rose, but grows upon a briar;
 sweet is the juniper, but sharp his bough;
 sweet is the eglantine, but pricketh near;
 sweet is the firbloom, but his branches rough.
Sweet is the cypress, but his rind is tough;
 sweet is the nut, but bitter is his pill;
 sweet is the broom-flower, but yet sour enough;
 and sweet is moly, but his root is ill.
So every sweet with sour is tempered still,
 that maketh it be coveted the more;
 for easy things that may be got at will
 most sorts of men do set but little store.
Why then should I account of little pain,
 that endless pleasure shall unto me gain?

Like as a ship that through the ocean wide
 by conduct of some star doth make her way,
 whenas a storm hath dimmed her trusty guide
 out of her course doth wander far astray:
So I whose star, that wont with her bright ray
 me to direct, with clouds is overcast,
 do wander now in darkness and dismay
 through hidden perils round about me placed.
Yet hope I well that when this storm is past
 my Helice, the lodestar of my life,
 will shine again, and look on me at last,
 with lovely light to clear my cloudy grief.
Till then I wander, care-full, comfortless,
 in secret sorrow and sad pensiveness.

Helice: Elisé, Elizabeth, his wife—with a reference to Helicon. The legendary Helice was beloved by Zeus, transformed by jealous Hera into a she-bear, and by Zeus again into the constellation, the Great Bear.

My hungry eyes through greedy covetise
    still to behold the object of their pain
    with no contentment can themselves suffice,
    but, having, pine, and having not, complain.
For lacking it they cannot life sustain,
    and having it they gaze on it the more,
    in their amazement like Narcissus vain
    whose eyes him starved: so plenty makes me poor.
Yet are mine eyes so fillèd with the store
    of that fair sight, that nothing else they brook,
    but loathe the things which they did like before,
    and can no more endure on them to look.
All this world's glory seemeth vain to me,
    and all their shows but shadows, saving she.

What guile is this, that those her golden tresses
    she doth attire under a net of gold,
    and with sly skill so cunningly them dresses
    that which is gold or hair may scarce be told?
Is it that men's frail eyes, which gaze too bold,
    she may entangle in that golden snare,
    and being caught may craftily enfold
    their weaker hearts, which are not well aware?
Take heed therefore, mine eyes, how ye do stare
    henceforth too rashly on that guileful net,
    in which if ever ye entrappèd are,
    out of her bands ye by no means shall get.
Fondness it were for any being free
    to cover fetters, though they golden be.

Sweet smile, the daughter of the Queen of Love,
    expressing all thy mother's powerful art,
    with which she wonts to temper angry Jove
    when all the gods he threats with thundering dart.
Sweet is thy virtue as thyself sweet art,
    for when on me thou shinedst late in sadness,
    a melting pleasance ran through every part,
    and me revivèd with heart-robbing gladness.
Whilst rapt with joy resembling heavenly madness,
    my soul was ravished quite as in a trance,
    and feeling thence no more her sorrow's sadness,
    fed on the fulness of that cheerful glance,
More sweet than nectar or ambrosial meat
    seemed every bit which thenceforth I did eat.

Thrice happy she that is so well assured
    unto herself and settled so in heart
    that neither will for better be allured
    ne feared with worse to any chance to start;
But like a steady ship doth strongly part
    the raging waves and keeps her course aright,
    ne ought for tempest doth from it depart,
    ne ought for fairer weather's false delight.
Such self-assurance need not fear the spite
    of grudging foes, ne favour seek of friends;
    but in the stay of her own steadfast might
    neither to one herself nor other bends.
Most happy she that most assured doth rest,
    but he most happy who such one loves best.

The glorious image of the Maker's beauty,
    my sovereign saint, the idol of my thought,
    dare not henceforth above the bounds of duty
    to accuse of pride, or rashly blame for ought.
For being as she is divinely wrought,
    and of the brood of angels heavenly born,
    and with the crew of blessèd Saints up-brought,
    each of which did her with their gifts adorn;
The bud of joy, the blossom of the morn,
    the beam of light, whom mortal eyes admire;
    what reason is it then that she should scorn
    base things that to her love too bold aspire?
Such heavenly forms ought rather worshipped be
    than dare be loved by men of low degree.

After long storms' and tempests' sad assay,
    which hardly I endurèd heretofore;
    in dread of death and dangerous dismay,
    with which my silly bark was tossèd sore,
I do at length descry the happy shore,
    in which I hope ere long for to arrive;
    fair soil it seems from far and fraught with store
    of all that dear and dainty is alive.
Most happy he that can at last achieve
    the joyous safety of so sweet a rest;
    whose least delight sufficeth to deprive
    remembrance of all pains which him oppressed.
All pains are nothing in respect of this,
    all sorrows short that gain eternal bliss.

Like as a huntsman after weary chase,
   seeing the game from him escapt away,
   sits down to rest him in some shady place,
   with panting hounds beguilèd of their prey:
So after long pursuit and vain assay,
   when I all weary had the chase forsook,
   the gentle deer returned the self-same way,
   thinking to quench her thirst at the next brook.
There she, beholding me with milder look,
   sought not to fly, but fearless still did bide;
   till I in hand her yet half trembling took,
   and with her own goodwill her firmly tied.
Strange thing, me seemed, to see a beast so wild,
   so goodly won, with her own will beguiled.

Most glorious Lord of life, that on this day
   didst make thy triumph over death and sin;
   and having harrowed hell, didst bring away
   captivity thence captive, us to win:
This joyous day, dear Lord, with joy begin,
   and grant that we for whom thou diddest die,
   being with thy dear blood clean washed from sin,
   may live for ever in felicity:
And that thy love we, weighing worthily,
   may likewise love thee for the same again;
   and for thy sake that all like dear didst buy,
   with love may one another entertain.
So let us love, dear love, like as we ought:
   love is the lesson which the Lord us taught.

Oft when my spirit doth spread her bolder wings,
    in mind to mount up to the purest sky,
    it down is weighed with thought of earthly things
    and clogged with burden of mortality;
Where when that sovereign beauty it doth spy,
    resembling heaven's glory in her light,
    drawn with sweet pleasure's bait, it back doth fly
    and unto heaven forgets her former flight.
There my frail fancy, fed with full delight,
    doth bathe in bliss, and mantleth most at ease;
    ne thinks of other heaven, but how it might
    her heart's desire with most contentment please.
Heart need not wish none other happiness
    but here on earth to have such heaven's bliss.

One day I wrote her name upon the strand,
    but came the waves and washèd it away:
    again I wrote it with a second hand,
    but came the tide, and made my pains his prey.
Vain man! said she, that dost in vain assay
    a mortal thing so to immortalize;
    for I myself shall like to this decay,
    and eke my name be wipèd out likewise.
Not so, quoth I; let baser things devise
    to die in dust, but you shall live by fame:
    my verse your virtues rare shall eternize,
    and in the heavens write your glorious name.
Where, whenas death shall all the world subdue,
    our love shall live, and later life renew.

mantleth: stretches its wings for exercise.

Fair is my Love, when her fair golden hairs
    with the loose wind ye waving chance to mark;
    fair, when the rose in her red cheeks appears,
    or in her eyes the fire of love does spark.
Fair when her breast, like a rich-laden bark
    with precious merchandise, she forth doth lay;
    fair when that cloud of pride, which oft doth dark
    her goodly light, with smiles she drives away.
But fairest she when so she doth display
    the gate with pearls and rubies richly dight
    through which her words so wise do make their way
    to bear the message of her gentle sprite.
The rest be works of natures' wonderment,
    but this the work of heart's astonishment.

Joy of my life, full oft for loving you
    I bless my lot that was so lucky placed;
    but then the more your own mishap I rue,
    that are so much by so mean love embased.
For had the equal heavens so much you graced
    in this as in the rest, ye mote invent
    some heavenly wit whose verse could have enchased
    your glorious name in golden moniment.
But since ye deigned so goodly to relent
    to me your thrall, in whom is little worth,
    that little that I am shall all be spent
    in setting your immortal praises forth:
Whose lofty argument, uplifting me,
    shall lift you up unto an high degree.

        mote: would have to.   moniment: record, memorial.

EDMUND SPENSER

Like as the culver on the barèd bough
   sits mourning for the absence of her mate;
   and in her songs sends many a wishful vow
   for his return that seems to linger late.
So I alone now left disconsolate
   mourn to myself the absence of my love;
   and wandring here and there all desolate
   seek with my plaints to match that mournful dove:
Ne joy of aught that under heaven doth hove
   can comfort me, but her own joyous sight,
   whose sweet aspect both God and man can move,
   in her unspotted pleasance to delight.
Dark is my day whiles her fair light I miss,
   and dead my life that wants such lively bliss.

SIR WALTER RALEGH

A Vision upon the Faery Queen

Methought I saw the grave where Laura lay,
Within that temple where the vestal flame
Was wont to burn; and passing by that way
To see that buried dust of living fame,
Whose tomb fair Love and fairer Virtue kept,
All suddenly I saw the Faery Queen:
At whose approach the soul of Petrarch wept;
And from thenceforth those Graces were not seen,
For they this Queen attended; in whose stead
Oblivion laid him down on Laura's hearse.
Hereat the hardest stones were seen to bleed,
And groans of buried ghosts the heavens did pierce,
   Where Homer's sprite did tremble all for grief,
   And cursed the access of that celestial thief.

culver: dove.   Laura: a woman loved by Petrarch.
Faery Queen: Queen Elizabeth.

18

Concerning the Honour of Books

Since honour from the honourer proceeds,
How well do they deserve, that memorize
And leave in Books for all posterities
The names of worthies and their virtuous deeds,
When all their glory else, like water-weeds
Without their element, presently dies,
And all their greatness quite forgotten lies,
And when and how they flourished no man heeds!
How poor remembrances are statues, tombs,
And other monuments that men erect
To princes, which remain in closèd rooms
Where but a few behold them, in respect
   Of Books, that to the universal eye
   Show how they lived; the other where they lie!

SIR PHILIP SIDNEY

Loving in truth, and fain in verse my love to show,
That She, dear She! might take some pleasure of my pain;
Pleasure might cause her read, reading might make her
    know,
Knowledge might pity win, and pity grace obtain:
I sought fit words to paint the blackest face of woe,
Studying inventions fine, her wits to entertain;
Oft turning others' leaves, to see if thence would flow
Some fresh and fruitful showers upon my sunburnt brain:
But words came halting forth, wanting Invention's stay.
Invention, Nature's child, fled step-dame Study's blows;
And others' feet still seemed but strangers in my way.
Thus great with child to speak, and helpless in my throes,
   Biting my truant pen, beating myself for spite,
   'Fool!' said my Muse to me, 'look in thy heart, and write!'

Let dainty wits cry on the Sisters nine,
That bravely maskt their fancies may be told;
Or Pindar's apes flaunt they in phrases fine,
Enamelling with pied flowers their thoughts of gold;
Or else let them in statelier glory shine,
Ennobling new-found tropes with problems old;
Or with strange similes enrich each line,
Of herbs or beasts which Ind or Afric hold:
   For me, in sooth, no Muse but one I know.
Phrases and problems from my reach do grow,
And strange things cost too dear for my poor sprites.
How then? Even thus. In Stella's face I read
What love and beauty be. Then all my deed
But copying is what in her Nature writes.

It is most true—that eyes are formed to serve
The inward light; and that the heavenly part
Ought to be King, from whose rules who doth swerve
(Rebels to Nature) strive for their own smart:
It is most true—what we call Cupid's dart
An image is which for ourselves we carve
And, fools! adore, in temple of our heart,
Till that good God make church and churchman starve:
True—that true beauty Virtue is indeed,
Whereof this beauty can be but a shade,
Which elements with mortal mixture breed:
True—that on earth we are but pilgrims made,
   And should in soul up to our country move:
   True—and yet true, that I must Stella love.

Pindar's apes: would-be imitators of Pindar, the Greek poet.

You that do search for every purling spring
Which from the ribs of old Parnassus flows;
And every flower, not sweet perhaps, which grows
Near thereabouts into your poesy wring;
You that no dictionary's method bring
Into your rhymes running in rattling rows;
You that poor Petrarch's long deceasèd woes
With newborn sighs and denizened wit do sing;
    You take wrong ways! Those far-fet helps be such
As do betray a want of inward touch;
And sure at length stol'n goods do come to light.
But if (both for your love and skill) your name
You seek to nurse at fullest breasts of Fame,
Stella behold, and then begin to endite.

His mother dear, Cupid offended late
Because that Mars, grown slacker in her love,
With pricking shot he did not throughly move
To keep the pace of their first loving state.
The boy refused for fear of Mars' hate,
Who threatened stripes if he his wrath did prove;
But she, in chafe, him from her lap did shove,
Break bow, break shafts, while weeping Cupid sate,
    Till that his grandame Nature pitying it,
Of Stella's brows made him two better bows,
And in her eyes, of arrows infinite.
O how for joy he leaps! O how he crows!
    And straight therewith—like wags new got to play—
    Falls to shrewd turns; and I was in his way.

With what sharp checks I in myself am shent
When into Reason's audit I do go;
And by just counts myself a bankrupt know
Of all those goods which heaven to me hath lent;
Unable quite to pay even Nature's rent,
Which unto it by birthright I do owe;
And, which is worse, no good excuse can show,
But that my wealth I have most idly spent.
My youth dost waste, my knowledge brings forth toys,
My wit doth strive those passions to defend
Which for reward spoil it with vain annoys.
I see my course to lose myself doth bend;
   I see, and yet no greater sorrow take
   Than that I lose no more for Stella's sake.

The curious wits, seeing dull pensiveness
Betray itself in my long-settled eyes,
Whence those same fumes of melancholy rise,
With idle pains and missing aim, do guess.
   Some that know how my Spring I did address
Deem that my Muse some fruit of knowledge plies;
Others, because the Prince my service tries,
Think that I think State errors to redress.
   But harder judges judge ambition's rage—
Scourge of itself, still climbing slippery place—
Holds my young brain captived in golden cage.
   O fools! or overwise! alas, the race
Of all my thoughts hath neither stop nor start
But only Stella's eyes and Stella's heart.

shent: rebuked.

Though dusty wits dare scorn astrology;
And fools can think those lamps of purest light—
Whose number, ways, greatness, eternity,
Promising wonders, wonder do invite—
 To have for no cause birthright in the sky,
But for to spangle the black weeds of Night;
Or for some brawl, which in that chamber high,
They should still dance to please a gazer's sight.
 For me, I do nature unidle know,
And know great causes great effects procure,
And know those bodies high reign on the low;
 And if these rules did fail, proof makes me sure,
Who oft fore-judge my after-following race
By only those two stars in Stella's face.

Whether the Turkish new moon minded be
To fill his horns this year on Christian coast?
How Poles' right King means, without leave of host,
To warm with ill-made fire cold Muscovy?
If French can yet three parts in one agree?
What now the Dutch in their full diets boast?
How Holland's hearts—now so good towns be lost—
Trust in the shade of pleasing Orange tree?
How Ulster likes of that same golden bit
Wherewith my father once made it half tame?
If in the Scotch Court be no welt'ring yet?
These questions busy wits to me do frame:
 I—cumbered with good manners—answer do,
 But know not how, for still I think on you.

With how sad steps, O Moon! thou climb'st the skies!
How silently! and with how wan a face!
What! may it be that even in heavenly place
That busy archer his sharp arrows tries?
    Sure, if that long-with-love-acquainted eyes
Can judge of love, thou feel'st a lover's case.
I read it in thy looks. Thy languisht grace
To me that feel the like thy state descries.
    Then even of fellowship, O Moon! tell me
Is constant love deemed there but want of wit?
Are beauties there as proud as here they be?
Do they above love to be loved, and yet
Those lovers scorn whom that love doth possess?
Do they call virtue there ungratefulness?

Morpheus! the lively son of deadly Sleep,
Witness of life to them that living die.
A prophet oft, and oft an history,
A poet eke; as humours fly and creep:
    Since thou in me so sure a power dost keep
That never I with close up sense do lie
But by thy work my Stella I descry,
Teaching blind eyes both how to smile and weep.
    Vouchsafe of all acquaintance this to tell!
Whence hast thou ivory, rubies, pearl and gold,
To show her skin, lips, teeth and head so well?
    'Fool!' answers he, 'no Inds such treasures hold;
But from thy heart, while my sire charmeth thee,
Sweet Stella's image I do steal to me.'

I might—unhappy word, O me!—I might,
And then would not, or could not see my bliss;
Till now, wrapt in a most infernal night,
I find how heavenly day, wretch! I did miss.
    Heart rend thyself! thou dost thyself but right.
No lovely Paris made thy Helen his;
No force, no fraud, robbed thee of thy delight;
No fortune of thy fortune author is;
    But to myself, myself did give the blow;
While too much wit (forsooth!) so troubled me
That I respects for both our sakes must show:
    And yet could not by rising morn foresee
How fair a day was near. O punished eyes!
That I had been more foolish or more wise!

Come, let me write. 'And to what end?' To ease
A burthened heart. 'How can words ease, which are
The glasses of thy daily vexing care?'
Oft, cruel fights well pictured forth do please.
    'Art not ashamed to publish thy disease?'
Nay that may breed my fame. It is so rare.
'But will not wise men think thy words fond ware?'
Then be they close, and so none shall displease.
    'What idler thing, than speak and not be heard?'
What harder thing, than smart and not to speak?
'Peace! foolish wit!' With wit my wit is marred.
    Thus write I, while I doubt to write; and wreak
My harms on ink's poor loss. Perhaps some find
Stella's great powers, that so confuse my mind.

Having this day my horse, my hand, my lance
Guided so well that I obtained the prize,
Both by the judgment of the English eyes
And of some sent by that sweet enemy, France!
    Horsemen my skill in horsemanship advance;
Townsfolk, my strength; a daintier judge applies
His praise to sleight which from good use doth rise;
Some lucky wits impute it but to chance;
    Others, because, of both sides, I do take
My blood from them who did excel in this,
Think Nature me a man-at-arms did make.
    How far they shot awry! The true cause is,
Stella lookt on, and from her heavenly face
Sent forth the beams which made so fair my race.

Fair eyes! sweet lips! dear heart! that foolish I
Could hope, by Cupid's help, on you to prey,
Since to himself he doth your gifts apply
As his main force, choice sport, and easeful stay.
    For when he will see who dare him gainsay,
Then with those eyes he looks. Lo! by and by
Each soul doth at Love's feet his weapons lay,
Glad if for her he give them leave to die.
    When he will play, then in her lips he is,
Where blushing red, that Love's self them doth love,
With either lip he doth the other kiss.
    But when he will for quiet's sake remove
From all the world, her heart is then his room,
Where, well he knows, no man to him can come.

Come Sleep! O Sleep! the certain knot of peace!
The baiting place of wit! the balm of woe!
The poor man's wealth! the prisoner's release!
Th'indifferent judge between the high and low!
    With shield of proof, shield me from out the press
Of those fierce darts Despair at me doth throw!
O make in me those civil wars to cease!
I will good tribute pay if thou do so.
    Take thou of me smooth pillows, sweetest bed,
A chamber deaf to noise and blind to light,
A rosy garland, and a weary head:
    And if these things as being thine by right
Move not thy heavy Grace, thou shalt in me
Livelier than elsewhere, Stella's image see.

Because I breathe not love to every one,
Nor do not use set colours for to wear,
Nor nourish special locks of vowèd hair,
Nor give each speech a full point of a groan,
    The courtly nymphs, acquainted with the moan
Of them who in their lips Love's standard bear;
'What he!' say they of me, 'now I dare swear
He cannot love. No, no, let him alone!'
    And think so still! so Stella know my mind.
Profess indeed I do not Cupid's art;
But you, fair maids! at length this true shall find:
    That his right badge is but worn in the heart.
Dumb swans, not chattering pies, do lovers prove.
They love indeed who quake to say they love.

Oft with true sighs, oft with uncallèd tears,
Now with slow words, now with dumb eloquence,
I Stella's eyes assailed, invade her ears;
But this at last is her sweet breathed defence.
    'That who indeed infelt affection bears,
So captives to his saint both soul and sense
That, wholly hers, all selfness he forbears:
Thence his desires he learns, his life's course thence.'
    Now since her chaste mind hates this love in me,
With chastened mind I needs must show that she
Shall quickly me from what she hates remove.
    O Doctor Cupid! thou for me reply!
Driven else to grant by angel's sophistry
That I love not, without I leave to love.

No more! my Dear! no more these counsels try!
O give my passions leave to run their race!
Let Fortune lay on me her worst disgrace!
Let folk o'ercharged with brain against me cry!
    Let clouds bedim my face, break in mine eye!
Let me no steps but of lost labour trace!
Let all the earth in scorn recount my case,
But do not will me from my love to fly!
    I do not envy Aristotle's wit,
Nor do aspire to Caesar's bleeding fame,
Nor aught do care though some above me sit,
    Nor hope, nor wish, another course to frame;
But that which once may win thy cruel heart.
Thou art my Wit, and thou my Virtue art.

And do I see some cause a hope to feed?
Or doth the tedious burden of long woe
In weakened minds quick apprehending breed
Of every image which may comfort show?
    I cannot brag of word, much less of deed;
Fortune's wheel's still with me in one sort slow;
My wealth no more, and no whit less my need:
Desire still on the stilts of fear doth go.
    And yet amid all fears, a hope there is
Stolen to my heart, since last fair night (nay, day!)
Stella's eyes sent to me the beams of bliss,
    Looking on me, while I lookt other way:
But when mine eyes back to their heaven did move,
They fled with blush which guilty seemed of love.

O joy! too high for my low style to show.
O bliss! fit for a nobler seat than me.
Envy! put out thine eyes! lest thou do see
What oceans of delight in me do flow.
    My friend! that oft saw, through all masks, my woe,
Come! come! and let me pour myself on thee!
Gone is the winter of my misery!
My spring appears! O see what here doth grow!
    For Stella hath with words (where faith doth shine)
Of her high heart given me the monarchy:
I! I! O I may say that she is mine.
    And though she give but thus conditionally
This realm of bliss, 'while virtuous course I take,'
No kings be crowned but they some covenant make.

I never drank of Aganippe's well,
Nor never did in shade of Tempe sit;
And Muses scorn with vulgar brains to dwell.
Poor layman, I! for sacred rites unfit.

Some do, I hear, of poets' fury tell;
But (God wot) wot not what they mean by it:
And this I swear by blackest brook of hell,
I am no pick-purse of another's wit.

How falls it then, that with so smooth an ease
My thoughts I speak? and what I speak doth flow
In verse? and that my verse best wits doth please?

Guess we the cause. What, is it thus? Fie, no!
Or so? Much less! How then? Sure thus it is.
My lips are sweet, inspired with Stella's kiss.

Good brother Philip I have borne you long.
I was content you should in favour creep,
While craftily you seemed your cut to keep;
As though that fair soft hand did you great wrong.

I bare (with envy) yet I bare your song,
When in her neck you did love ditties peep;
Nay, more fool I! oft suffered you to sleep
In lilies' nest, where Love's self lies along.

What! doth high place ambitious thoughts augment?
Is sauciness reward of courtesy?
Cannot such grace your silly self content,

But you must needs with those lips billing be?
And through those lips drink nectar from that tongue?
Leave that Sir Phip! lest off your neck be wrung!

Aganippe: a nymph of the fountain so called, at the foot of Mount Helicon. The fountain was sacred to the Muses, and could inspire those who
drank from it.

Tempe: a delightful valley in Thessaly, frequently described by the
ancient poets.

cut: luck, fortune.

Highway! since you my chief Parnassus be,
And that my Muse to some ears not unsweet
Tempers her words to trampling horses' feet
More oft than to a chamber melody.

Now blessèd you! bear onward blessèd me
To her, where I my heart safeliest shall meet.
My Muse and I must you of duty greet
With thanks and wishes, wishing thankfully.

Be you still fair! honoured by public heed!
By no encroachment wronged! nor time forgot!
Nor blamed for blood, nor shamed for sinful deed!

And that you know I envy you no lot
Of highest wish, I wish you so much bliss:
Hundreds of years you Stella's feet may kiss!

Stella! think not that I by verse seek fame,
Who seek, who hope, who love, who live but thee.
Thine eyes my pride; thy lips mine history:
If thou praise not, all other praise is shame.

Not so ambitious am I as to frame
A nest for my young praise in laurel tree:
In truth I swear I wish not there should be
Graved in my epitaph a Poet's name.

Ne if I would I could just title make
That any laud to me thereof should grow,
Without my plumes from others' wings I take.

For nothing from my wit or will doth flow,
Since all my words thy beauty doth endite,
And love doth hold my hand and makes me write.

Since Nature's works be good, and death doth serve
As Nature's work, why should we fear to die?
Since fear is vain but when it may preserve,
Why should we fear that which we cannot fly?
    Fear is more pain than is the pain it fears,
Disarming human minds of native might;
While each conceit an ugly feature bears
Which were not evil, well viewed in reason's light.
    Our owly eyes, which dimmed with passions be,
And scarce discern the dawn of coming day,
Let them be cleared, and now begin to see
Our life is but a step in dusty way.
    Then let us hold the bliss of peaceful mind;
    Since this we feel, great loss we cannot find.

Leave me, O Love, which reachest but to dust,
And thou, my mind, aspire to higher things.
Grow rich in that which never taketh rust.
Whatever fades, but fading pleasure brings.
Draw in thy beams, and humble all thy might
To that sweet yoke where lasting freedoms be,
Which breaks the clouds and opens forth the light
That doth both shine and give us sight to see.
    O take fast hold! Let that light be thy guide
In this small course which birth draws out to death:
And think how evil becometh him to slide
Who seeketh heaven, and comes of heavenly breath.
    Then farewell, world! thy uttermost I see.
    Eternal Love, maintain Thy life in me.

Thou blind man's mark, thou fool's self-chosen snare,
Fond fancy's scum, and dregs of scattered thought;
Band of all evils, cradle of causeless care,
Thou web of will, whose end is never wrought:
Desire! Desire! I have too dearly bought,
With price of mangled mind, thy worthless ware;
Too long, too long, asleep thou hast me brought,
Who should my mind to higher things prepare.
    But yet in vain thou hast my ruin sought;
In vain thou mad'st me to vain things aspire;
In vain thou kindlest all thy smoky fire;
For Virtue hath this better lesson taught,—
Within myself to seek my only hire,
Desiring nought but how to kill Desire.

Be your words made, good sir, of Indian ware,
That you allow me them by so small rate?
Or do you cutted Spartans imitate?
Or do you mean my tender ears to spare
That to my questions you so total are?
When I demand of Phoenix Stella's state,
You say, forsooth, you left her well of late:
O God, think you that satisfies my care?
    I would know whether she did sit or walk;
How clothed; how waited on; sighed she or smiled;
Whereof, with whom, how often did she talk;
With what pastime time's journey she beguiled;
If her lips deigned to sweeten my poor name:
Say all; and, all well said, still say the same.

cutted: curt, laconic.

Seed-time and Harvest

The nurse-life wheat within his green husk growing
Flatters our hopes and tickles our desire;
Nature's true riches in sweet beauties showing,
Which set all hearts with labour's love on fire.
No less fair is the wheat when golden ear
Shows unto hope the joys of near enjoying:
Fair and sweet is the bud; more sweet and fair
The rose, which proves that Time is not destroying.
Caelica, your youth, the morning of delight,
Enamelled o'er with beauties white and red,
All sense and thoughts did to belief invite,
That love and glory there are brought to bed;
　　And your ripe years, Love, now they grow no higher,
　　Turn all the spirits of man into desire.

JOHN LYLY

Cupid and Campaspë

Cupid and my Campaspë played
At cards for kisses; Cupid paid:
He stakes his quiver, bow, and arrows,
His mother's doves, and team of sparrows;
Loses them too; then down he throws
The coral of his lip, the rose
Growing on's cheek (but none knows how);
With these, the crystal of his brow,
And then the dimple of his chin:
All these did my Campaspë win.
At last he set her both his eyes—
She won, and Cupid blind did rise.
　　O Love! has she done this for thee?
　　What shall, alas! become of me?

34

THOMAS WATSON

I saw the object of my pining thought
Within a garden of sweet Nature's placing,
Wherein an arbour artificial wrought,
By workman's wondrous skill the garden gracing,
Did boast his glory, glory far renowned,
For in his shady boughs my mistress slept,
And with a garland of his branches crowned,
Her dainty forehead from the sun ykept.
Imperious Love upon her eyelids tending,
Playing his wanton sports at every beck,
And into every finest limb descending,
From eyes to lips, from lips to ivory neck;
    And every limb supplied, and t'every part
     Had free access, but durst not touch her heart.

BARTHOLOMEW GRIFFIN

Venus, and young Adonis sitting by her,
Under a myrtle shade, began to woo him;
She told the youngling how god Mars did try her,
And as he fell to her, so fell she to him.
'Even thus,' quoth she, 'the wanton god embraced me!'
And then she clasped Adonis in her arms;
'Even thus,' quoth she, 'the warlike god unlaced me!'
As if the boy should use like loving charms.
But he, a wayward boy, refused the offer,
And ran away, the beauteous queen neglecting;
Showing both folly to abuse her proffer,
And all his sex of cowardice detecting.
    O that I had my mistress at that bay,
    To kiss and clip me till I ran away!

clip: embrace.

35

Fair is my Love that feeds among the lilies,
The lilies growing in that pleasant garden
Where Cupid's Mount that well belovèd hill is,
And where that little god himself is warden.
See where my Love sits in the beds of spices,
Beset all round with camphor, myrrh, and roses,
And interlaced with curious devices
Which her apart from all the world incloses!
There doth she tune her lute for her delight,
And with sweet music makes the ground to move,
Whilst I, poor I, do sit in heavy plight,
Wailing alone my unrespected love:
 Not daring rush into so rare a place,
 That gives to her, and she to it, a grace.

THOMAS LODGE

How languisheth the primrose of Love's garden!
 How trill her tears, the elixir of my senses!
 Ambitious sickness, what doth thee so harden?
 Oh spare, and plague thou me for her offences!
Ah roses, love's fair roses, do not languish;
 Blush through the milk-white veil that holds you
  covered.
 If heat or cold may mitigate your anguish,
 I'll burn, I'll freeze, but you shall be recovered.
Good God, would beauty mark how she is crazed,
 How but one shower of sickness makes her tender,
 Her judgements then, to mark my woes amazed,
 To mercy should opinion's fort surrender.
And I, oh would I might, or would she meant it!
Should herry love, who now in heart lament it.

herry: praise.

ROBERT GREENE

Ah! were she pitiful as she is fair,
Or but as mild as she is seeming so
Then were my hopes greater than my despair,
Then all the world were heaven, nothing woe.
Ah! were her heart relenting as her hand,
That seems to melt even with the mildest touch,
Then knew I where to seat me in a land
Under wide heavens; but yet there is none such.
So as she shows she seems the budding rose,
Yet sweeter far than is an earthly flower;
Sov'ran of beauty, like the spray she grows;
Compassed she is with thorns and cankered bower.
    Yet were she willing to be plucked and worn,
    She would be gathered, though she grew on thorn.

SAMUEL DANIEL

Look, Delia, how we 'steem the half-blown rose
    (The image of thy blush, and summer's honour),
    Whilst in her tender green she doth inclose
    The pure sweet beauty Time bestows upon her.
No sooner spreads her glory in the air,
    But straight her full-blown pride is in declining;
    She then is scorned that late adorned the fair:
    So clouds thy beauty, after fairest shining.
No April can revive thy withered flowers,
    Whose blooming grace adorns thy glory now;
    Swift speedy Time, feathered with flying hours,
    Dissolves the beauty of the fairest brow.
O let not then such riches waste in vain,
But love, whilst that thou may'st be loved again.

Care-charmer Sleep, son of the sable Night,
    Brother to Death, in silent darkness born:
    Relieve my languish, and restore the light;
    With dark forgetting of my care return,
And let the day be time enough to mourn
    The shipwreck of my ill-adventured youth:
    Let waking eyes suffice to wail their scorn
    Without the torment of the night's untruth.
Cease, dreams, the images of day desires,
    To model forth the passions of the morrow;
    Never let rising sun approve you liars,
    To add more grief to aggravate my sorrow.
Still let me sleep, embracing clouds in vain,
And never wake to feel the day's disdain.

Let others sing of Knights and Paladins,
    In aged accents, and intimely words,
    Paint shadows, in imaginary lines,
    Which well the reach of their high wits records.
But I must sing of thee; and those fair eyes
    Authentic shall my verse in time to come,
    When yet the unborn shall say, Lo, where she lies
    Whose beauty made him speak, that else was dumb.
These are the arks, the trophies I erect,
    That fortify thy name against old age;
    And these thy sacred virtues must protect
    Against the dark, and Time's consuming rage.
Though th'error of my youth, they shall discover;
Suffice they show I lived, and was thy lover.

When men shall find thy flower, thy glory, pass;
    And thou, with care-full brow, sitting alone,
    Receivèd hast this message from thy glass,
    That tells the truth and says that all is gone;
Fresh shalt thou see in me the wounds thou madest,
    Though spent thy flame, in me the heat remaining.
    I that have loved thee thus before thou fadest,
    My faith shall wax, when thou art in thy waning.
The world shall find this miracle in me,
    That fire can burn when all the matter's spent.
    Then what my faith hath been thyself shalt see,
    And that thou wast unkind thou may'st repent.
Thou may'st repent that thou hast scorned my tears,
When winter snows upon thy sable hairs.

And yet I cannot reprehend the flight,
    Or blame th'attempt, presuming so to soar:
    The mounting venture for a high delight
    Did make the honour of the fall the more.
For who gets wealth, that puts not from the shore?
    Danger hath honour, great designs their fame;
    Glory doth follow, courage goes before;
    And though th'event oft answers not the same,
Suffice that high attempts have never shame.
    The mean-observer (whom base safety keeps)
    Lives without honour, dies without a name,
    And in eternal darkness ever sleeps.
And therefore, Delia, 'tis to me no blot
To have attempted, though attained thee not.

Beauty, sweet love, is like the morning dew,
　　Whose short refresh upon the tender green
　　Cheers for a time, but till the sun doth show;
　　And straight 'tis gone, as it had never been.
Soon doth it fade, that makes the fairest flourish;
　　Short is the glory of the blushing rose;
　　The hue which thou so carefully dost nourish,
　　Yet which, at length, thou must be forced to lose,
When thou, surcharged with burden of thy years,
　　Shalt bend thy wrinkles homeward to the earth,
　　When Time hath made a passport for thy fears,
　　Dated in age, the kalends of our death.
But, ah! no more! This hath been often told;
And women grieve to think they must be old.

HENRY CONSTABLE

To Sir Philip Sidney's Soul

Give pardon, blessèd soul, to my bold cries
　　If they, importune, interrupt thy song
　　Which now with joyful notes thou singst among
　　The angel-quiristers of heavenly skies.
Give pardon eke, sweet soul, to my slow cries,
　　That since I saw thee now it is so long,
　　And yet the tears that unto thee belong,
　　To thee as yet they did not sacrifice:
I did not know that thou wert dead before,
　　I did not feel the grief I did sustain;
　　The greater stroke astonisheth the more,
　　Astonishment takes from us sense of pain:
I stood amazed when others' tears begun,
And now begin to weep, when they have done.

Were I as base as is the lowly plain,
And you, my Love, as high as heaven above,
Yet should the thoughts of me your humble swain
Ascend to heaven in honour of my love.
Were I as high as heaven above the plain,
And you, my Love, as humble and as low
As are the deepest bottoms of the main,
Wheresoe'er you were, with you my love should go.
Were you the earth, dear Love, and I the skies,
My love should shine on you like to the sun,
And look upon you with ten thousand eyes,
Till heaven waxed blind, and till the world were done.
    Wheresoe'er I am, below, or else above you,
    Wheresoe'er you are, my heart shall truly love you

They say that shadows of deceasèd ghosts
Do haunt the houses and the graves about,
Of such whose life's lamp went untimely out,
Delighting still in their forsaken hosts:
So, in the place where cruel Love doth shoot
The fatal shaft that slew my love's delight,
I stalk, and walk, and wander day and night,
Even like a ghost with unperceivèd foot.
But those light ghosts are happier far than I,
For, at their pleasure, they can come and go
Unto the place that hides their treasure so,
And see the same with their fantastic eye:
    Where I, alas, dare not approach the cruel
    Proud monument that doth enclose my jewel.

Fra bank to bank, fra wood to wood I rin,
　　Ourhailit with my feeble fantasie;
　　Like til a leaf that fallis from a tree,
Or til a reed ourblawin with the win.

Twa gods guides me: the ane of tham is blin,
　　Yea and a bairn brocht up in vanitie;
　　The next a wife ingenrit of the sea,
And lichter nor a dauphin with her fin.

Unhappy is the man for evermair
That tills the sand and sawis in the air;
　　But twice unhappier is he, I lairn,
That feidis in his hairt a mad desire,
And follows on a woman throw the fire,
　　Led by a blind and teachit by a bairn.

MICHAEL DRAYTON

How many paltry foolish painted things
That now in coaches trouble every street
Shall be forgotten (whom no poet sings)
Ere they be well wrapped in their winding sheet!
　　Where I to thee eternity shall give
When nothing else remaineth of these days:
And queens hereafter shall be glad to live
Upon the alms of thy superfluous praise.
　　Virgins and matrons, reading these my rhymes,
Shall be so much delighted with thy story
That they shall grieve they lived not in these times,
To have seen thee, their sex's only glory.
　　So shalt thou fly above the vulgar throng,
　　Still to survive in my immortal song.

ourhailit: overwhelmed.

42

There's nothing grieves me, but that age should haste,
That in my days I may not see thee old:
That where those two clear sparkling eyes are placed,
Only two loopholes then I might behold:
    That lovely archèd ivory-polished brow
Defaced with wrinkles that I might but see:
Thy dainty hair, so curled and crispèd now,
Like grizzled moss upon some aged tree:
    Thy cheek, now flush with roses, sunk and lean,
Thy lips, with age, as any wafer thin,
Thy pearly teeth out of thy head so clean
That when thou feed'st, thy nose shall touch thy chin.
    These lines that now thou scornst, which should delight
      thee,
    Then would I make thee read, but to despite thee.

To nothing fitter can I thee compare
Than to the son of some rich penny-father
Who having now brought on his end with care,
Leaves to his son all he had heaped together.
    This new rich novice, lavish of his chest,
To one man gives, doth on another spend;
Then here he riots, yet, among the rest,
Haps to lend some to one true honest friend.
    Thy gifts thou in obscurity dost waste,
False friends thy kindness, born but to deceive thee;
Thy love, that is on the unworthy placed;
Time hath thy beauty, which with age will leave thee.
    Only that little which to me was lent
    I give thee back when all the rest is spent.

An evil spirit (your beauty) haunts me still,
Wherewith, alas, I have been long possessed,
Which ceaseth not to tempt me to each ill,
Nor give me once but one poor minute's rest.

In me it speaks whether I sleep or wake;
And when by means to drive it out I try,
With greater torments then it me doth take,
And tortures me in most extremity.

Before my face it lays down its despairs,
And hastes me on unto a sudden death;
Now tempting me to drown myself in tears,
And then in sighing to give up my breath.

Thus am I still provoked to every evil
By this good-wicked spirit, sweet angel-devil.

A witless gallant a young wench that wooed
(Yet his dull spirit her not one jot could move),
Entreated me, as e'er I wished his good,
To write him but one sonnet to his Love;

When I, as fast as e'er my pen could trot,
Poured out what first from quick invention came,
Nor ever stood one word thereof to blot,
Much like his wit that was to use the same.

But with my verses he his mistress won,
Who doated on the dolt beyond all measure.
But see: for you to heaven for phrase I run,
And ransack all Apollo's golden treasure;

Yet by my froth this fool his Love obtains,
And I lose you, for all my wit and pains.

Love, banished heaven, in earth was held in scorn,
Wandering abroad in need and beggary,
And wanting friends, though of a goddess born,
Yet craved the alms of such as passèd by.

I, like a man devout and charitable,
Clothèd the naked, lodged this wandering guest,
With sighs and tears still furnishing his table
With what might make the miserable blest.

But this ungrateful, for my good desert,
Enticed my thoughts against me to conspire;
Who gave consent to steal away my heart,
And set my breast (his lodging) on a fire.

Well, well, my friends, when beggars grow thus bold,
No marvel then though charity grow cold.

To the Critics

Methinks I see some crooked mimic jeer
And tax my muse with this fantastic grace;
Turning my papers, asks What have we here?
Making withal some filthy antic face.

I fear no censure, nor what thou canst say;
Nor shall my spirit one jot of vigour lose.
Think'st thou my wit shall keep the packhorse way
That every dudgeon low invention goes?

Since sonnets thus in bundles are imprest,
And every drudge doth dull our satiate ear,
Think'st thou my Love shall in those rags be drest
That every dowdy, every trull, doth wear?

Up to my pitch no common judgement flies.
I scorn all earthly dung-bred scarabies.

To Admiration

Marvel not, Love, though I thy power admire,
Ravished a world beyond the farthest thought,
And knowing more than ever hath been taught,
That I am only starved in my desire:
    Marvel not, Love, though I thy power admire,
Aiming at things exceeding all perfection,
To wisdom's self to minister direction,
That I am only starved in my desire:
    Marvel not, Love, though I thy power admire,
Though my conceit I further seem to bend
Than possibly invention can extend,
And yet am only starved in my desire:
    If thou wilt wonder, here's the wonder, Love:
    That this to me doth yet no wonder prove.

Dear, why should you command me to my rest,
When now the night doth summon all to sleep?
Methinks this time becometh lovers best:
Night was ordained together friends to keep.
    How happy are all other living things
Which, through the day disjoined by several flight,
The quiet evening yet together brings,
And each returns unto his Love at night.
    O thou that art so courteous else to all,
Why shouldst thou, Night, abuse me only thus,
That every creature to his kind dost call,
And yet 'tis thou dost only sever us?
    Well could I wish it would be ever day,
    If, when night comes, you bid me go away.

Some men there be which like my method well,
And much commend the strangeness of my vein.
Some say I have a passing pleasant strain,
Some say that in my humour I excel.
　　Some, who not kindly relish my conceit,
They say as poets do I use to feign,
And in bare words paint out my passion's pain.
Thus sundry men their sundry minds repeat.
　　I pass not, I, how men affected be,
Nor who commends or discommends my verse.
It pleaseth me if I my woes rehearse,
And in my lines if She my love may see.
　　Only my comfort still consists in this:
　　Writing her praise I cannot write amiss.

Whilst thus my pen strives to eternize thee,
Age rules my lines with wrinkles in my face,
Where, in the map of all my misery,
Is modelled out the world of my disgrace.
　　Whilst in despite of tyrannizing times,
Medea-like, I make thee young again,
Proudly thou scorn'st my world-outwearing rhymes
And murder'st virtue with thy coy disdain.
　　And though in youth my youth untimely perish,
To keep thee from oblivion and the grave,
Ensuing ages yet my rhymes shall cherish,
Where I, entombed, my better part shall save;
　　And though this earthly body fade and die,
　　My name shall mount upon eternity.

As in some countries far remote from hence
The wretched creature destinèd to die,
Having the judgement due to his offence,
By surgeons begged, their art on him to try;
    Which, on the living, work without remorse,
First make incision on each mastering vein,
Then staunch the bleeding, then transpierce the corse,
And with their balms recure the wound again.
    Then poison and with physic him restore;
Not that they fear the hopeless man to kill,
But their experience to increase the more:—
Even so my mistress works upon my ill,
    By curing me and killing me each hour,
    Only to show her beauty's sovereign power.

To Proverbs

As Love and I late harboured in one inn,
With proverbs thus each other entertain.
In love there is no lack thus I begin:
Fair words make fools replieth he again.
    Who spares to speak doth spare to speed quoth I:
As well saith he *too forward as too slow.*
Fortune assists the boldest I reply:
A hasty man quoth he *ne'er wanted woe.*
    Labour is light where love quoth I *doth pay:*
Saith he *Light burden's heavy if far borne.*
Quoth I *The main lost, cast the bye away.*
You have spun a fair thread he replies in scorn.
    And having thus awhile each other thwarted,
    Fools as we met, so fools again we parted.

MICHAEL DRAYTON

Since there's no help, come, let us kiss and part.
Nay, I have done. You get no more of me.
And I am glad, yea, glad with all my heart,
That thus so cleanly I myself can free.
    Shake hands for ever, cancel all our vows,
And when we meet at any time again
Be it not seen in either of our brows
That we one jot of former love retain.
    Now at the last gasp of Love's fleeting breath,
When, his pulse failing, Passion speechless lies,
When Faith is kneeling by his bed of death,
And Innocence is closing up his eyes,
    Now, if thou wouldst, when all have given him over,
    From death to life thou might'st him yet recover.

CHARLES BEST

A Sonnet of the Moon

Look how the pale queen of the silent night
Doth cause the ocean to attend upon her,
And he, as long as she is in his sight,
With his full tide is ready her to honour;
But when the silver waggon of the moon
Is mounted up so high he cannot follow,
The sea calls home his crystal waves to moan,
And with low ebb doth manifest his sorrow.
So you, that are the sovereign of my heart,
Have all my joys attending on your will;
My joys low-ebbing when you do depart,
When you return, their tide my heart doth fill:
    So as you come and as you do depart,
    Joys ebb and flow within my tender heart.

When forty winters shall besiege thy brow
And dig deep trenches in thy beauty's field,
Thy youth's proud livery, so gazed on now
Will be a tattered weed, of small worth held:
Then being asked where all thy beauty lies,
Where all the treasure of thy lusty days,
To say, within thine own deep-sunken eyes,
Were an ill-eating shame and thriftless praise.
How much more praise deserved thy beauty's use,
If thou couldst answer 'This fair child of mine
Shall sum my count and make my old excuse,'
Proving his beauty by succession thine!
 This were to be new made when thou art old,
 And see thy blood warm when thou feel'st it cold.

When I do count the clock that tells the time,
And see the brave day sunk in hideous night;
When I behold the violet past prime,
And sable curls all silvered o'er with white;
When lofty trees I see barren of leaves,
Which erst from heat did canopy the herd,
And summer's green all girded up in sheaves,
Borne on the bier with white and bristly beard,
Then of thy beauty do I question make,
That thou among the wastes of time must go,
Since sweets and beauties do themselves forsake,
And die as fast as they see others grow;
 And nothing 'gainst Time's scythe can make defence
 Save breed, to brave him when he takes thee hence.

Shall I compare thee to a summer's day?
Thou art more lovely and more temperate:
Rough winds do shake the darling buds of May,
And summer's lease hath all too short a date:
Sometime too hot the eye of heaven shines,
And often is his gold complexion dimmed;
And every fair from fair sometime declines,
By chance or nature's changing course untrimmed;
But thy eternal summer shall not fade,
Nor lose possession of that fair thou owest;
Nor shall Death brag thou wander'st in his shade,
When in eternal lines to time thou growest:
    So long as men can breathe, or eyes can see,
    So long lives this, and this gives life to thee.

As an unperfect actor on the stage,
Who with his fear is put beside his part,
Or some fierce thing replete with too much rage,
Whose strength's abundance weakens his own heart;
So I, for fear of trust, forget to say
The perfect ceremony of love's rite,
And in mine own love's strength seem to decay,
O'ercharged with burthen of mine own love's might.
O, let my books be then the eloquence
And dumb presagers of my speaking breast;
Who plead for love, and look for recompense,
More than that tongue that more hath more exprest.
    O, learn to read what silent love hath writ;
    To hear with eyes belongs to love's fine wit.

When, in disgrace with fortune and men's eyes,
I all alone beweep my outcast state,
And trouble deaf heaven with my bootless cries,
And look upon myself, and curse my fate,
Wishing me like to one more rich in hope,
Featured like him, like him with friends possest
Desiring this man's art and that man's scope,
With what I most enjoy contented least;
Yet in these thoughts myself almost despising,
Haply I think on thee, and then my state,
Like to the lark at break of day arising
From sullen earth, sings hymns at heaven's gate;
    For thy sweet love remembered such wealth brings
    That then I scorn to change my state with kings.

When to the sessions of sweet silent thought
I summon up remembrance of things past,
I sigh the lack of many a thing I sought,
And with old woes new wail my dear time's waste:
Then can I drown an eye, unused to flow,
For precious friends hid in death's dateless night,
And weep afresh love's long since cancelled woe,
And moan the expense of many a vanished sight:
Then can I grieve at grievances foregone,
And heavily from woe to woe tell o'er
The sad account of fore-bemoanèd moan,
Which I new pay as if not paid before.
    But if the while I think on thee, dear friend,
    All losses are restored and sorrows end.

Thy bosom is endearèd with all hearts
Which I by lacking have supposèd dead;
And there reigns love, and all love's loving parts,
And all those friends which I thought burièd.
How many a holy and obsequious tear
Hath dear religious love stol'n from mine eye,
As interest of the dead, which now appear
But things removed that hidden in thee lie!
Thou art the grave where buried love doth live,
Hung with the trophies of my lovers gone,
Who all their parts of me to thee did give:
That due of many now is thine alone:
    Their images I loved I view in thee,
    And thou, all they, hast all the all of me.

If thou survive my well-contented day
When that churl Death my bones with dust shall cover,
And shalt by fortune once more re-survey
These poor rude lines of thy deceasèd lover,
Compare them with the bettering of the time,
And though they be outstript by every pen,
Reserve them for my love, not for their rhyme,
Exceeded by the height of happier men.
O, then vouchsafe me but this loving thought:
'Had my friend's Muse grown with this growing age,
A dearer birth than this his love had brought,
To march in ranks of better equipage:
    But since he died, and poets better prove,
    Theirs for their style I'll read, his for his love.'

Full many a glorious morning have I seen
Flatter the mountain-tops with sovereign eye,
Kissing with golden face the meadows green,
Gilding pale streams with heavenly alchemy;
Anon permit the basest clouds to ride
With ugly rack on his celestial face,
And from the forlorn world his visage hide,
Stealing unseen to west with this disgrace:
Even so my sun one early morn did shine
With all-triumphant splendour on my brow;
But, out, alack! he was but one hour mine,
The region cloud hath maskt him from me now.
 Yet him for this my love no whit disdaineth;
 Suns of the world may stain when heaven's sun staineth.

Mine eye and heart are at a mortal war,
How to divide the conquest of thy sight;
Mine eye my heart thy picture's sight would bar,
My heart mine eye the freedom of that right.
My heart doth plead that thou in him dost lie,
A closet never pierced with crystal eyes,
But the defendant doth that plea deny,
And says in him thy fair appearance lies.
To 'cide this title is impannelèd
A quest of thoughts, all tenants to the heart;
And by their verdict is determinèd
The clear eye's moiety and the dear heart's part;
 As thus; mine eye's due is thy outward part,
 And my heart's right thy inward love of heart.

So am I as the rich, whose blessèd key
Can bring him to his sweet up-lockèd treasure,
The which he will not every hour survey,
For blunting the fine point of seldom pleasure.
Therefore are feasts so solemn and so rare,
Since, seldom coming, in the long year set,
Like stones of worth they thinly placèd are,
Or captain jewels in the carcanet.
So is the time that keeps you, as my chest,
Or as the wardrobe which the robe doth hide,
To make some special instant special blest,
By new unfolding his imprisoned pride.
   Blessèd are you, whose worthiness gives scope,
   Being had, to triumph, being lackt, to hope.

O, how much more doth beauty beauteous seem
By that sweet ornament which truth doth give!
The rose looks fair, but fairer we it deem
For that sweet odour which doth in it live.
The canker-blooms have full as deep a dye
As the perfumed tincture of the roses,
Hang on such thorns, and play as wantonly
When summer's breath their maskèd buds discloses:
But, for their virtue only is their show,
They live unwooed, and unrespected fade;
Die to themselves. Sweet roses do not so;
Of their sweet deaths are sweetest odours made:
   And so of you, beauteous and lovely youth,
   When that shall vade, my verse distills your truth.

carcanet: necklace.   vade: fade.

Not marble, nor the gilded monuments
Of princes, shall outlive this powerful rhyme;
But you shall shine more bright in these contents
Than unswept stone, besmeared with sluttish time.
When wasteful war shall statues overturn,
And broils root out the work of masonry,
Nor Mars his sword nor war's quick fire shall burn
The living record of your memory.
'Gainst death and all-oblivious enmity
Shall you pace forth; your praise shall still find room
Even in the eyes of all posterity
That wear this world out to the ending doom.
   So, till the judgement, that yourself arise,
   You live in this, and dwell in lovers' eyes.

Being your slave, what should I do but tend
Upon the hours and times of your desire?
I have no precious time at all to spend,
Nor services to do, till you require.
Nor dare I chide the world-without-end hour
Whilst I, my sovereign, watch the clock for you,
Nor think the bitterness of absence sour
When you have bid your servant once adieu;
Nor dare I question with my jealous thought
Where you may be, or your affairs suppose,
But, like a sad slave, stay and think of nought
Save, where you are how happy you make those.
   So true a fool is love that in your will
   Though you do any thing, he thinks no ill.

Like as the waves make towards the pebbled shore,
So do our minutes hasten to their end;
Each changing place with that which goes before,
In sequent toil all forwards do contend.
Nativity, once in the main of light,
Crawls to maturity, wherewith being crowned,
Crooked eclipses 'gainst his glory fight,
And Time that gave doth now his gift confound.
Time doth transfix the flourish set on youth,
And delves the parallels in beauty's brow,
Feeds on the rarities of nature's truth;
And nothing stands but for his scythe to mow:
    And yet to times in hope my verse shall stand,
    Praising thy worth, despite his cruel hand.

When I have seen by Time's fell hand defaced
The rich-proud cost of outworn buried age;
When sometime lofty towers I see down-razed,
And brass eternal slave to mortal rage;
When I have seen the hungry ocean gain
Advantage on the kingdom of the shore
And the firm soil win of the watery main,
Increasing store with loss and loss with store;
When I have seen such interchange of state,
Or state itself confounded to decay;
Ruin hath taught me thus to ruminate,
That Time will come and take my Love away.
    This thought is as a death, which cannot choose
    But weep to have that which it fears to lose.

main: full force.

Since brass, nor stone, nor earth, nor boundless sea,
But sad mortality o'er-sways their power,
How with this rage shall beauty hold a plea,
Whose action is no stronger than a flower?
O, how shall summer's honey breath hold out
Against the wrackful siege of battering days,
When rocks impregnable are not so stout,
Nor gates of steel so strong, but Time decays?
O fearful meditation! where, alack,
Shall Time's best jewel from Time's chest lie hid?
Or what strong hand can hold his swift foot back?
Or who his spoil of beauty can forbid?
 O, none, unless this miracle have might,
 That in black ink my love may still shine bright.

Tired with all these, for restful death I cry,
As, to behold desert a beggar born,
And needy nothing trimmed in jollity,
And purest faith unhappily forsworn,
And gilded honour shamefully misplaced,
And maiden virtue rudely strumpeted,
And right perfection wrongfully disgraced,
And strength by limping sway disabled,
And art made tongue-tied by authority,
And folly, doctor-like, controlling skill,
And simple truth miscalled simplicity,
And captive good attending captain ill:
 Tired with all these, from these would I be gone,
 Save that, to die, I leave my Love alone.

chest: Theobald read "quest;" but see the first sonnet on p. 55.

That thou art blamed shall not be thy defect,
For slander's mark was ever yet the fair;
The ornament of beauty is suspect,
A crow that flies in heaven's sweetest air.
So thou be good, slander doth but approve
Thy worth the greater, being wooed of time;
For canker vice the sweetest buds doth love,
And thou present'st a pure unstainèd prime.
Thou hast passed by the ambush of young days,
Either not assailed, or victor being charged;
Yet this thy praise cannot be so thy praise,
To tie up envy evermore enlarged:
    If some suspect of ill maskt not thy show,
    Then thou alone kingdoms of hearts shouldst owe.

No longer mourn for me when I am dead
Than you shall hear the surly sullen bell
Give warning to the world that I am fled
From this vile world, with vilest worms to dwell:
Nay, if you read this line, remember not
The hand that writ it; for I love you so,
That I in your sweet thoughts would be forgot,
If thinking on me then should make you woe.
O, if, I say, you look upon this verse
When I perhaps compounded am with clay,
Do not so much as my poor name rehearse,
But let your love even with my life decay;
    Lest the wise world should look into your moan,
    And mock you with me after I am gone.

That time of year thou mayst in me behold
When yellow leaves, or none, or few, do hang
Upon those boughs which shake against the cold,
Bare ruined choirs, where late the sweet birds sang.
In me thou see'st the twilight of such day
As after sunset fadeth in the west;
Which by and by black night doth take away,
Death's second self, that seals up all in rest.
In me thou see'st the glowing of such fire,
That on the ashes of his youth doth lie,
As the death-bed whereon it must expire,
Consumed with that which it was nourisht by.
   This thou perceivest, which makes thy love more strong,
    To love that well which thou must leave ere long.

Was it the proud full sail of his great verse,
Bound for the prize of all-too-precious you,
That did my ripe thoughts in my brain inhearse,
Making their tomb the womb wherein they grew?
Was it his spirit, by spirits taught to write
Above a mortal pitch, that struck me dead?
No, neither he, nor his compeers by night
Giving him aid, my verse astonishèd.
He, nor that affable familiar ghost
Which nightly gulls him with intelligence,
As victors, of my silence cannot boast;
I was not sick of any fear from thence:
   But when your countenance filled up his line,
    Then lackt I matter; that enfeebled mine.

Farewell! thou art too dear for my possessing,
And like enough thou know'st thy estimate:
The charter of thy worth gives thee releasing;
My bonds in thee are all determinate.
For how do I hold thee but by thy granting?
And for that riches where is my deserving?
The cause of this fair gift in me is wanting,
And so my patent back again is swerving.
Thyself thou gavest, thy own worth then not knowing,
Or me, to whom thou gavest it, else mistaking;
So thy great gift, upon misprision growing,
Comes home again, on better judgement making.
    Thus have I had thee, as a dream doth flatter,
    In sleep a king, but waking no such matter.

Then hate me when thou wilt; if ever, now;
Now, while the world is bent my deeds to cross,
Join with the spite of fortune, make me bow,
And do not drop in for an after-loss:
Ah, do not, when my heart hath 'scaped this sorrow,
Come in the rearward of a conquered woe;
Give not a windy night a rainy morrow,
To linger out a purposed overthrow.
If thou wilt leave me, do not leave me last,
When other petty griefs have done their spite,
But in the onset come: so shall I taste
At first the very worst of fortune's might;
    And other strains of woe, which now seem woe,
    Compared with loss of thee will not seem so.

Some glory in their birth, some in their skill,
Some in their wealth, some in their body's force;
Some in their garments, though new-fangled ill;
Some in their hawks and hounds, some in their horse;
And every humour hath his adjunct pleasure,
Wherein it finds a joy above the rest:
But these particulars are not my measure;
All these I better in one general best.
Thy love is better than high birth to me,
Richer than wealth, prouder than garments' cost,
Of more delight than hawks or horses be;
And having thee, of all men's pride I boast:
 Wretched in this alone, that thou mayst take
 All this away, and me most wretched make.

They that have power to hurt and will do none,
That do not do the thing they most do show,
Who, moving others, are themselves as stone,
Unmovèd, cold and to temptation slow;
They rightly do inherit heaven's graces
And husband nature's riches from expense;
They are the lords and owners of their faces,
Others but stewards of their excellence.
The summer's flower is to the summer sweet,
Though to itself it only live and die,
But if that flower with base infection meet,
The basest weed outbraves his dignity:
 For sweetest things turn sourest by their deeds;
 Lilies that fester smell far worse than weeds.

How like a winter hath my absence been
From thee, the pleasure of the fleeting year!
What freezings have I felt, what dark days seen!
What old December's bareness everywhere!
And yet this time removed was summer's time;
The teeming autumn, big with rich increase,
Bearing the wanton burthen of the prime,
Like widowed wombs after their lord's decease:
Yet this abundant issue seemed to me
But hope of orphans and unfathered fruit;
For summer and his pleasures wait on thee,
And, thou away, the very birds are mute;
    Or, if they sing, 'tis with so dull a cheer
    That leaves look pale, dreading the winter's near.

From you have I been absent in the spring,
When proud-pied April, drest in all his trim,
Hath put a spirit of youth in every thing,
That heavy Saturn laught and leapt with him.
Yet nor the lays of birds, nor the sweet smell
Of different flowers in odour and in hue,
Could make me any summer's story tell,
Or from their proud lap pluck them where they grew:
Nor did I wonder at the lily's white,
Nor praise the deep vermilion in the rose;
They were but sweet, but figures of delight,
Drawn after you, you pattern of all those.
    Yet seemed it winter still, and, you away,
    As with your shadow I with these did play.

My love is strengthened, though more weak in seeming;
I love not less, though less the show appear:
That love is merchandized whose rich esteeming
The owner's tongue doth publish every where.
Our love was new, and then but in the spring,
When I was wont to greet it with my lays;
As Philomel in summer's front doth sing,
And stops her pipe in growth of riper days:
Not that the summer is less pleasant now
Than when her mournful hymns did hush the night,
But that wild music burthens every bough,
And sweets grown common lose their dear delight.
　　Therefore, like her, I sometime hold my tongue,
　　Because I would not dull you with my song.

To me, fair friend, you never can be old,
For as you were when first your eye I eyed,
Such seems your beauty still. Three winters cold
Have from the forests shook three summers' pride,
Three beauteous springs to yellow autumn turned
In process of the seasons have I seen,
Three April perfumes in three hot Junes burned,
Since first I saw you fresh, which yet are green.
Ah, yet doth beauty, like a dial-hand,
Steal from his figure, and no pace perceived;
So your sweet hue, which methinks still doth stand,
Hath motion, and mine eye may be deceived:
　　For fear of which, hear this, thou age unbred;
　　Ere you were born was beauty's summer dead.

When in the chronicle of wasted time
I see descriptions of the fairest wights,
And beauty making beautiful old rhyme
In praise of ladies dead and lovely knights,
Then, in the blazon of sweet beauty's best,
Of hand, of foot, of lip, of eye, of brow,
I see their antique pen would have exprest
Even such a beauty as you master now.
So all their praises are but prophecies
Of this our time, all you prefiguring;
And, for they lookt but with divining eyes,
They had not skill enough your worth to sing:
    For we, which now behold these present days,
    Have eyes to wonder, but lack tongues to praise.

Not mine own fears, nor the prophetic soul
Of the wide world dreaming on things to come,
Can yet the lease of my true love control,
Supposed as forfeit to a confined doom.
The mortal moon hath her eclipse endured,
And the sad augurs mock their own presage;
Incertainties now crown themselves assured,
And peace proclaims olives of endless age.
Now with the drops of this most balmy time
My love looks fresh, and Death to me subscribes,
Since, spite of him, I'll live in this poor rhyme,
While he insults o'er dull and speechless tribes:
    And thou in this shalt find thy monument,
    When tyrants' crests and tombs of brass are spent.

insults: exults.

O, never say that I was false of heart,
Though absence seemed my flame to qualify.
As easy might I from myself depart
As from my soul, which in thy breast doth lie:
That is my home of love: if I have ranged,
Like him that travels I return again;
Just to the time, not with the time exchanged,
So that myself bring water for my stain.
Never believe, though in my nature reigned
All frailties that besiege all kinds of blood,
That it could so preposterously be stained,
To leave for nothing all thy sum of good;
     For nothing this wide universe I call,
     Save thou, my rose; in it thou art my all.

Alas, 'tis true I have gone here and there,
And made myself a motley to the view,
Gored mine own thoughts, sold cheap what is most dear,
Made old offences of affections new;
Most true it is that I have lookt on truth
Askance and strangely: but, by all above,
These blenches gave my heart another youth,
And worse essays proved thee my best of love.
Now all is done, have what shall have no end:
Mine appetite I never more will grind
On newer proof, to try an older friend,
A god in love, to whom I am confined.
     Then give me welcome, next my heaven the best,
     Even to thy pure and most loving breast.

O, for my sake do you with Fortune chide,
The guilty goddess of my harmful deeds,
That did not better for my life provide
Than public means which public manners breeds.
Thence comes it that my name receives a brand,
And almost thence my nature is subdued
To what it works in, like the dyer's hand:
Pity me then and wish I were renewed;
Whilst, like a willing patient, I will drink
Potions of eisel 'gainst my strong infection;
No bitterness that I will bitter think,
Nor double penance, to correct correction.
    Pity me then, dear friend, and I assure ye
    Even that your pity is enough to cure me.

Those lines that I before have writ do lie,
Even those that said I could not love you dearer:
Yet then my judgement knew no reason why
My most full flame should afterwards burn clearer.
But reckoning Time, whose millioned accidents
Creep in 'twixt vows, and change decrees of kings,
Tan sacred beauty, blunt the sharp'st intents,
Divert strong minds to the course of altering things;
Alas, why, fearing of Time's tyranny,
Might I not then say 'Now I love you best,'
When I was certain o'er incertainty,
Crowning the present, doubting of the rest?
    Love is a babe; then might I not say so,
    To give full growth to that which still doth grow?

eisel: vinegar.

Let me not to the marriage of true minds
Admit impediments. Love is not love
Which alters when it alteration finds,
Or bends with the remover to remove:
O, no! it is an ever-fixèd mark,
That looks on tempests and is never shaken;
It is the star to every wandering bark,
Whose worth's unknown, although his height be taken.
Love's not Time's fool, though rosy lips and cheeks
Within his bending sickle's compass come;
Love alters not with his brief hours and weeks,
But bears it out even to the edge of doom.
    If this be error, and upon me proved,
    I never writ, nor no man ever loved.

What potions have I drunk of Siren tears,
Distilled from limbecks foul as hell within,
Applying fears to hopes and hopes to fears,
Still losing when I saw myself to win!
What wretched errors hath my heart committed,
Whilst it hath thought itself so blessèd never!
How have mine eyes out of their spheres been fitted,
In the distraction of this madding fever!
O benefit of ill! now I find true
That better is by evil still made better;
And ruined love, when it is built anew,
Grows fairer than at first, more strong, far greater.
    So I return rebuked to my content,
    And gain by ill thrice more than I have spent.

No, Time, thou shalt not boast that I do change:
Thy pyramids built up with newer might
To me are nothing novel, nothing strange;
They are but dressings of a former sight.
Our dates are brief, and therefore we admire
What thou dost foist upon us that is old;
And rather make them born to our desire
Than think that we before have heard them told.
Thy registers and thee I both defy,
Not wondering at the present nor the past,
For thy records and what we see doth lie,
Made more or less by thy continual haste.
    This I do vow, and this shall ever be,
    I will be true, despite thy scythe and thee.

The expense of spirit in a wate of shame
Is lust in action; and till action, lust
Is perjured, murderous, bloody, full of blame,
Savage, extreme, rude, cruel, not to trust;
Enjoyed no sooner but despisèd straight;
Past reason hunted; and no sooner had,
Past reason hated, as a swallowed bait,
On purpose laid to make the taker mad:
Mad in pursuit, and in possession so;
Had, having, and in quest to have, extreme;
A bliss in proof, and proved, a very woe;
Before, a joy proposed; behind, a dream.
    All this the world well knows; yet none knows well
    To shun the heaven that leads men to this hell.

My mistress' eyes are nothing like the sun;
Coral is far more red than her lips' red:
If snow be white, why then her breasts are dun;
If hairs be wires, black wires grow on her head.
I have seen roses damaskt red and white,
But no such roses see I in her cheeks;
And in some perfumes is there more delight
Than in the breath that from my mistress reeks.
I love to hear her speak, yet well I know
That music hath a far more pleasing sound:
I grant I never saw a goddess go;
My mistress, when she walks, treads on the ground:
   And yet, by heaven, I think my love as rare
   As any she belied with false compare.

Lo, as a careful housewife runs to catch
One of her feathered creatures broke away,
Sets down her babe, and makes all swift dispatch
In pursuit of the thing she would have stay;
Whilst her neglected child holds her in chase,
Cries to catch her whose busy care is bent
To follow that which flies before her face,
Not prizing her poor infant's discontent:
So runn'st thou after that which flies from thee,
Whilst I thy babe chase thee afar behind;
But if thou catch thy hope, turn back to me,
And play the mother's part, kiss me, be kind:
   So will I pray that thou mayst have thy Will,
   If thou turn back and my loud crying still.

Two loves I have of comfort and despair,
Which like two spirits do suggest me still:
The better angel is a man right fair,
The worser spirit a woman coloured ill.
To win me soon to hell, my female evil
Tempteth my better angel from my side,
And would corrupt my saint to be a devil,
Wooing his purity with her foul pride.
And whether that my angel be turned fiend
Suspect I may, yet not directly tell;
But being both from me, both to each friend,
I guess one angel in another's hell:
    Yet this shall I ne'er know, but live in doubt,
    Till my bad angel fire my good one out.

Poor soul, the centre of my sinful earth,
[Foiled by] these rebel powers that thee array,
Why dost thou pine within and suffer dearth,
Painting thy outward walls so costly gay?
Why so large cost, having so short a lease,
Dost thou upon thy fading mansion spend?
Shall worms, inheritors of this excess,
Eat up thy charge? is this thy body's end?
Then, soul, live thou upon thy servant's loss,
And let that pine to aggravate thy store;
Buy terms divine in selling hours of dross;
Within be fed, without be rich no more:
    So shalt thou feed on Death, that feeds on men,
    And Death once dead, there's no more dying then.

O me, what eyes hath Love put in my head,
Which have no correspondence with true sight!
Or, if they have, where is my judgement fled,
That censures falsely what they see aright?
If that be fair whereon my false eyes dote,
What means the world to say it is not so?
If it be not, then love doth well denote
Love's eye is not so true as all men's: no,
How can it? O, how can Love's eye be true,
That is so vext with watching and with tears?
No marvel, then, though I mistake my view;
The sun itself sees not till heaven clears.
    O cunning Love! with tears thou keep'st me blind,
    Lest eyes well-seeing thy foul faults should find.

THOMAS CAMPION

Thrice toss these oaken ashes in the air,
And thrice three times tie up this true love's knot;
Thrice sit you down in this enchanted chair,
And murmur soft, 'She will or she will not.'
Go burn these poisoned weeds in that blue fire,
This cypress gathered at a dead man's grave,
These screech-owl's feathers, and the prickling briar,
That all thy thorny cares an end may have.
Then come, you fairies, dance with me a round;
Dance in a circle, let my Love be centre;
Melodiously breathe an enchanted sound,
Melt her hard heart, that some remorse may enter.
    In vain are all the charms I can devise:
    She hath an art to break them with her eyes.

Thou shalt not love me, neither shall these eyes
Shine on my soul shrouded in deadly night.
Thou shalt not breathe on me thy spiceries
Nor rock me in thy quavers of delight.
Hold off thy hands, for I had rather die
Than have my life by thy coy touch reprieved.
Smile not on me, but frown thou bitterly;
Slay me outright: no lovers are long-lived.
As for those lips, reserved so much in store,
Their rosy verdure shall not meet with mine.
Withhold thy proud embracements evermore;
I'll not be swaddled in those arms of thine.
   Now show it if thou be a woman right:
   Embrace and kiss and love me in despite.

WILLIAM ALEXANDER, EARL OF STIRLING

I swear, Aurora, by thy starry eyes,
And by those golden locks whose lock none slips,
And by the coral of thy rosy lips,
And by the naked snows which beauty dyes;
I swear by all the jewels of thy mind,
Whose like yet never worldly treasure bought,
Thy solid judgement and thy generous thought,
Which in this darkened age have clearly shined;
I swear by those, and by my spotless love,
And by my secret yet most fervent fires,
That I have never nurst but chaste desires,
And such as modesty might well approve.
Then since I love those virtuous parts in thee,
Should'st thou not love this virtuous mind in me?

I envy not Endymion now no more,
Nor all the happiness his sleep did yield
While as Diana, straying through the field,
Suckt from his sleep-sealed lips balm for her sore:
Whilst I embraced the shadow of my death,
I dreaming did far greater pleasure prove,
And quaft with Cupid sugared draughts of love,
Then, Jove-like, feeding on a nectared breath.
Now judge which of us two might be most proud;
He got a kiss yet not enjoyed it right,
And I got none, yet tasted that delight
Which Venus on Adonis once bestowed:
He only got the body of a kiss,
And I the soul of it, which he did miss.

O if thou knew'st how thou thyself dost harm,
And dost prejudge thy bliss, and spoil my rest:
Then thou wouldst melt the ice out of thy breast,
And thy relenting heart would kindly warm.
O if thy pride did not our joys control,
What world of loving wonders should'st thou see!
For if I saw thee once transformed in me,
Then in thy bosom I would pour my soul,
Then all thy thoughts should in my visage shine.
And if that ought mischanced thou should'st not moan,
Nor bear the burthen of thy griefs alone;
No, I would have my share in what were thine.
And whilst we thus should make our sorrows one,
This happy harmony would make them none.

O now I think, and do not think amiss,
That the old philosophers were all but fools,
Who used such curious questions in their schools,
Yet could not apprehend the highest bliss.
Lo, I have learned in the academy of love
A maxim which they never understood:
To love and be beloved, this is the good
Which for most sov'reign all the world will prove.
That which delights us most must be our treasure:
And to what greater joy can one aspire
Than to possess all that he doth desire,
Whilst two united souls do melt in pleasure?
This is the greatest good can be invented,
That is so great it cannot be augmented.

BARNABY BARNES

. Ah, sweet Content, where is thy mild abode?
 Is it with shepherds and light-hearted swains
 Which sing upon the downs and pipe abroad,
 Tending their flocks and cattle on the plains?
Ah, sweet Content, where dost thou safely rest?
 In heaven, with angels which the praises sing
 Of Him that made, and rules at his behest
 The minds and hearts of every living thing?
Ah, sweet Content, where doth thine harbour hold?
 Is it in churches with religious men
 Which please the gods with prayers manifold,
 And in their studies meditate it then?
Whether thou dost in heaven or earth appear,
 Be where thou wilt, thou wilt not harbour here.

BARNABY BARNES

Ah me! how many ways have I assayed
    To win my mistress to my ceaseless suit.
    What endless means and prayers have I made
    To thy fair graces, ever deaf and mute.
At thy long absence, like an errand page,
    With sighs and tears long journeys did I make
    Through paths unknown, in tedious pilgrimage,
    And never slept, but always did awake.
And having found thee ruthless and unkind,
    Soft skinned, hard hearted; sweet looks, void of pity,
    Ten thousand furies ragèd in my mind,
Changing the tenour of my lovely ditty
    By whose enchanting saws and magic spell
    Thine hard indurate heart I must compel.

JOHN DONNE

At the round earth's imagined corners, blow
Your trumpets, angels, and arise, arise
From death, you numberless infinities
Of souls, and to your scattered bodies go,
All whom the flood did, and fire shall o'erthrow,
All whom war, dearth, age, agues, tyrannies,
Despair, law, chance, hath slain, and you whose eyes
Shall behold God, and never taste death's woe.
But let them sleep, Lord, and we mourn a space,
For, if above all these my sins abound,
'Tis late to ask abundance of thy grace
When we are there; here on this lowly ground
Teach me how to repent; for that's as good
As if thou'dst sealed my pardon with thy blood.

Death, be not proud, though some have called thee
Mighty and dreadful, for thou art not so,
For those whom thou think'st thou dost overthrow
Die not, poor Death, nor yet canst thou kill me.
From rest and sleep, which but thy pictures be,
Much pleasure; then from thee much more must flow;
And soonest our best men with thee do go,
Rest of their bones, and soul's delivery.
Thou art slave to Fate, Chance, kings, and desperate men,
And dost with poison, war, and sickness dwell;
And poppy, or charms, can make us sleep as well
And better than thy stroke: why swell'st thou then?
One short sleep past, we wake eternally,
And death shall be no more; Death, thou shalt die.

Batter my heart, three-personed God, for you
As yet but knock; breathe, shine, and seek to mend;
That I may rise and stand, o'erthrow me and bend
Your force to break, blow, burn, and make me new.
I, like an usurpt town, to another due,
Labour to admit you, but Oh, to no end;
Reason your viceroy in me, me should defend,
But is captived, and proves weak or untrue.
Yet dearly I love you, and would be loved fain,
But am betrothed unto your enemy:
Divorce me, untie, or break that knot again,
Take me to you, imprison me, for I,
Except you enthrall me, never shall be free;
Nor ever chaste, except you ravish me.

On Poet-Ape

Poor Poet-ape, that would be thought our chief,
    Whose works are e'en the frippery of wit,
From brocage is become so bold a thief,
    As we, the robbed, leave rage, and pity it.
At first he made low shifts, would pick and glean,
    Buy the reversion of old plays; now grown
To a little wealth, and credit of the scene,
    He takes up all, makes each man's wit his own,
And, told of this, he slights it. Tut, such crimes
    The sluggish gaping auditor devours;
He marks not whose 'twas first: and after-times
    May judge it to be his, as well as ours.
Fool, as if half-eyes will not know a fleece
From locks of wool, or shreds from the whole piece?

RICHARD BARNFIELD

To his Friend Maister R[ichard] L[ynch]

If music and sweet poetry agree,
As they must needs, the sister and the brother,
Then must the love be great 'twixt thee and me,
Because thou lov'st the one, and I the other.
Dowland to thee is dear, whose heavenly touch
Upon the lute doth ravish human sense;
Spenser to me, whose deep conceit is such
As, passing all conceit, needs no defence.
Thou lov'st to hear the sweet melodious sound
That Phoebus' lute, the queen of music, makes;
And I in deep delight am chiefly drown'd
Whenas himself to singing he betakes.
    One god is god of both, as poets feign;
    One knight loves both, and both in thee remain.

brocage: brokerage, dealing in second-hand wares.

Beauty and Majesty are fall'n at odds,
Th'one claims his cheek, the other claims his chin;
Then Virtue comes and puts her title in:
Quoth she, I make him like th'immortal Gods.
Quoth Majesty, I own his looks, his brow;
His lips, quoth Love, his eyes, his hair, is mine;
And yet, quoth Majesty, he is not thine;
I mix disdain with Love's congealed snow.
Ay, but, quoth Love, his locks are mine by right.
His stately gait is mine, quoth Majesty;
And mine, quoth Virtue, is his Modesty.
Thus as they strive about the heavenly wight
   At last the other two to Virtue yield
    The lists of Love, fought in fair Beauty's field.

EDMUND BOLTON

As withereth the primrose by the river,
As fadeth summer's sun from gliding fountains,
As vanisheth the light-blown bubble ever,
As melteth snow upon the mossy mountains:
So melts, so vanisheth, so fades, so withers,
The rose, the shine, the bubble, and the snow,
Of praise, pomp, glory, joy, which short life gathers,
Fair praise, vain pomp, sweet glory, brittle joy.
The withered primrose by the mourning river,
The faded summer's sun from weeping fountains,
The light-blown bubble, vanishèd for ever,
The molten snow upon the naked mountains,
   Are emblems that the treasures we uplay
    Soon wither, vanish, fade, and melt away.

For as the snow, whose lawn did overspread
The ambitious hills, which giant-like did threat
To pierce the heaven with their aspiring head,
Naked and bare doth leave their craggy seat:
When as the bubble, which did empty fly,
The dalliance of the undiscernèd wind,
On whose calm rolling waves it did rely,
Hath shipwreck made, where it did dalliance find:
And when the sunshine which dissolved the snow,
Coloured the bubble with a pleasant vary,
And made the rathe and timely primrose grow,
Swarth clouds withdraw, which longer time do tarry:
   O what is praise, pomp, glory, joy, but so
   As shine by fountains, bubbles, flowers or snow?

EDWARD LORD HERBERT OF CHERBURY

Lord, thus I sin, repent, and sin again,
   As if repentance only were, in me,
Leave for new sin; thus do I entertain
   My short time, and thy Grace, abusing thee
   And thy long-suffering; which though it be
Ne'er overcome by sin, yet were in vain
   If tempted oft: thus we our errors see
Before our punishment, and so remain
   Without excuse; and, Lord, in them 'tis true,
Thy laws are just, but why dost thou distrain
   Ought else for life, save life? That is thy due:
   The rest thou mak'st us owe, and mayst to us
As well forgive; but oh! my sins renew
   Whilst I do talk with my Creator thus.

rathe: blooming early in the year.

Of Black Beauty

Black beauty which, above that common light
 Whose power can no colours here renew
 But those which darkness can again subdue,
Dost still remain unvaried to the sight,
And like an object equal to the view
 Art neither changed with day, nor hid with night,
 When all these colours which the world call bright,
And which old poetry doth so pursue,
Are with the night so perishèd and gone
 That of their being there remains no mark,
Thou still abidest so entirely one,
 That we may know thy blackness is a spark
Of light inaccessible, and alone
 Our darkness which can make us think it dark.

To Black Itself

Thou Black, wherein all colours are composed,
 And unto which they all at last return,
 Thou colour of the sun where it doth burn,
And shadow, where it cools, in thee is closed
Whatever nature can, or hath disposed
 In any other hue: from thee do rise
Those tempers and complexions which, disclosed
 As part of thee, do work as mysteries
Of that thy hidden power; when thou dost reign,
 The characters of fate shine in the skies
And tell us what the heavens do ordain;
 But when earth's common light shines to our eyes,
Thou so retir'st thyself that thy disdain
 All revelation unto man denies.

Renownèd Spenser, lie a thought more nigh
To learned Chaucer, and rare Beaumont lie
A little nearer Spenser, to make room
For Shakespeare in your threefold, fourfold tomb.
To lodge all four in one bed, make a shift
Until Doomsday, for hardly will a fift
Betwixt this day and that by Fate be slain,
For whom your curtains may be drawn again.
If your precedency in death doth bar
A fourth place in your sacred sepulchre,
Under this carvèd marble of thine own
Sleep, rare tragedian, Shakespeare sleep alone;
Thy unmolested peace, unsharèd cave
Possess as lord, not tenant of thy grave.
    That unto us and others it may be
    Honour hereafter to be laid by thee.

WILLIAM DRUMMOND OF HAWTHORNDEN

In my first years, and prime not yet at height,
When sweet conceits my wits did entertain,
Ere beauty's force I knew or false delight,
Or to what oar she did her captives chain;
Led by a sacred troupe of Phoebus' train,
I first began to read, then love to write,
And so to praise a perfect red and white,
But (God wot) wist not what was in my brain:
Love smiled to see in what an awful guise
I turned those antiques of the age of gold,
And that I might more mysteries behold,
He set so fair a volume to mine eyes,
    That I (quires closed which, dead, dead sighs but breathe)
    Joy on this living book to read my death.

I know that all beneath the moon decays,
And what by mortals in this world is brought
In time's great periods shall return to nought;
That fairest states have fatal nights and days.
I know that all the Muses' heavenly lays,
With toil of sprite which are so dearly bought,
As idle sounds, of few, or none are sought,
And that nought lighter is than airy praise.
I know frail beauty like the purple flower
To which one morn oft birth and death affords;
That love a jarring is of mind's accords,
Where sense and will envassal reason's power:
    Know what I list, this all cannot me move
    But that, O me! I both must write and love.

Sleep, Silence' child, sweet father of soft rest,
Prince whose approach peace to all mortals brings,
Indifferent host to shepherds and to kings,
Sole comforter of minds with grief opprest:
Lo, by thy charming rod all breathing things
Lie slumbring, with forgetfulness possest,
And yet o'er me to spread thy drowsy wings
Thou spares, alas, who cannot be thy guest.
Since I am thine, O come, but with that face
To inward light which thou art wont to show,
With feignèd solace ease a true felt woe;
Or if, deaf god, thou do deny that grace,
    Come as thou wilt, and what thou wilt bequeath;
    I long to kiss the image of my death.

Then is she gone? O fool and coward I!
O good occasion lost, ne'er to be found!
What fatal chains have my dull senses bound,
When best they may, that they not fortune try?
Here is the fainting grass where she did lie,
With roses here she stellified the ground;
She fixt her eyes on this yet smiling pond,
Nor time nor courteous place seemed ought deny.
Too long, too long, Respect, I do embrace
Your counsel, full of threats and sharp disdain:
Disdain in her sweet heart can have no place,
And though come there, must straight retire again:
    Henceforth, Respect, farewell! I oft hear told,
    Who lives in love can never be too bold.

Dear quirister, who from those shadows sends,
Ere that the blushing dawn dare show her light,
Such sad lamenting strains, that night attends
Become all ear, stars stay to hear thy plight:
If one whose grief even reach of thought transcends,
Who ne'er, not in a dream, did taste delight,
May thee importune who like care pretends,
And seems to joy in woe, in woe's despite;
Tell me (so may thou fortune milder try,
And long, long sing) for what thou thus complains
Sith, winter gone, the sun in dappled sky
Now smiles on meadows, mountains, woods, and plains?
    The bird, as if my question did her move,
    With trembling wings sobbed forth, I love! I love!

If crost with all mishaps be my poor life,
If one short day I never spent in mirth,
If my sprite with itself holds lasting strife,
If sorrow's death is but new sorrow's birth;
If this vain world be but a sable stage,
Where slave-born man plays to the scoffing stars,
If youth be tost with love, with weakness age,
If knowledge serves to hold our thoughts in wars,
If time can close the hundred mouths of Fame,
And make what's long since past, like that's to be,
If virtue only be an idle name,
If being born I was but born to die;
    Why seek I to prolong these loathsome days?
    The fairest rose in shortest time decays.

Dear wood, and you sweet solitary place
Where from the vulgar I estrangèd live,
Contented more with what your shades me give
Than if I had what Thetis doth embrace:
What snaky eye grown jealous of my peace
Now from your silent horrors would me drive?
When sun, progressing in his glorious race
Beyond the Twins, doth near our pole arrive.
What sweet delight a quiet life affords,
And what it is to be from bondage free,
Far from the madding worldlings' hoarse discords,
Sweet flow'ry place I first did learn of thee:
    Ah! if I were mine own, your dear resorts
    I would not change with princes' stately courts.

My lute, be as thou wast when thou didst grow
With thy green mother in some shady grove,
When immelodious winds but made thee move,
And birds on thee their ramage did bestow.
Sith that dear voice which did thy sounds approve,
Which used in such harmonious strains to flow,
Is reft from earth to tune those spheres above,
What art thou but a harbinger of woe?
Thy pleasing notes be pleasing notes no more,
But orphan wailings to the fainting ear,
Each stop a sigh, each sound draws forth a tear;
Be therefore silent as in woods before,
   Or if that any hand to touch thee deign,
   Like widowed turtle, still her loss complain.

What doth it serve to see Sun's burning face,
And skies enamelled with both the Indies' gold,
Or moon at night in jetty chariot rolled,
And all the glory of that starry place?
What doth it serve earth's beauty to behold,
The mountains' pride, the meadows' flow'ry grace,
The stately comeliness of forests old,
The sport of floods which would themselves embrace?
What doth it serve to hear the Sylvans' songs,
The wanton merle, the nightingale's sad strains,
Which in dark shades seem to deplore my wrongs?
For what doth serve all that this world contains,
   Sith she for whom those once to me were dear
   No part of them can have now with me here?

ramage: the song of the birds (Fr. *ramage*).   merle: blackbird (Sc.).

To spread the azure canopy of heaven
And make it twinkle all with spangs of gold,
To place this pondrous globe of earth so even
That it should all, and nought should it uphold;
To give strange motions to the planets seven,
And Jove to make so meek, and Mars so bold,
To temper what is moist, dry, hot, and cold,
Of all their jars that sweet accords are given;
Lord, to thy wit is nought, nought to thy might;
But that thou shouldst, thy glory laid aside,
Come basely in mortality to bide,
And die for them deserved eternal plight,
   A wonder is, so far above our wit
   That angels stand amazed to think on it.

Look how the flower which lingeringly doth fade,
The morning's darling late, the summer's queen,
Spoiled of that juice which kept it fresh and green,
As high as it did raise, bows low the head:
Right so my life (contentments being dead,
Or in their contraries but only seen)
With swifter speed declines than erst it spread,
And, blasted, scarce now shows what it hath been.
As doth the pilgrim therefore whom the night
By darkness would imprison on his way,
Think on thy home, my soul, and think aright,
Of what yet rests thee of life's wasting day:
   Thy sun posts westward, passèd is thy morn,
   And twice it is not given thee to be born.

Of this fair volume which we World do name,
If we the sheets and leaves could turn with care,
Of Him who it corrects, and did it frame,
We clear might read the art and wisdom rare:
Find out his power which wildest pow'rs doth tame,
His providence extending everywhere,
His justice which proud rebels doth not spare,
In every page, no, period of the same:
But silly we, like foolish children, rest
Well pleased with coloured vellum, leaves of gold,
Fair dangling ribbons, leaving what is best,
On the great Writer's sense ne'er taking hold;
　　Or if by chance our minds do muse on ought,
　　It is some picture in the margin wrought.

For the Baptist

The last and greatest Herald of Heaven's King,
Girt with rough skins, hies to the deserts wild,
Among that savage brood the woods forth bring,
Which he than man more harmless found and mild:
His food was locusts, and what there doth spring,
With honey that from virgin hives distilled;
Parcht body, hollow eyes, some uncouth thing
Made him appear, long since from earth exiled.
There burst he forth: All ye whose hopes rely
On God, with me amidst these deserts mourn.
Repent, repent, and from old errors turn.
Who listened to his voice, obeyed his cry?
　　Only the echoes which he made relent
　　Rung from their flinty caves, Repent, repent.

To a Nightingale

Sweet bird that singst away the early hours,
Of winters past or coming void of care,
Well pleasèd with delights that present are,
Fair seasons, budding sprays, sweet-smelling flowers:
To rocks, to springs, to rills, from leavy bowers
Thou thy creator's goodness dost declare,
And what dear gifts on thee he did not spare,
A stain to human sense in sin that lowers.
What soul can be so sick, which by thy songs
Attired in sweetness, sweetly is not driven
Quite to forget earth's turmoils, spites, and wrongs,
And lift a reverent eye and thought to heaven?
    Sweet artless songster, thou my mind dost raise
    To airs of spheres, yes, and to angels' lays.

Doth then the world go thus, doth all thus move?
Is this the justice which on earth we find?
Is this that firm decree which all doth bind?
Are these your influences, powers above?
Those souls which vice's moody mists most blind,
Blind fortune blindly most their friend doth prove:
And they who thee, poor idol, virtue love
Ply like a feather tost by storm and wind.
Ah! if a providence doth sway this all,
Why should best minds groan under most distress,
Or why should pride humility turn thrall,
And injuries the innocent oppress?
    Heavens! hinder, stop this fate, or grant a time
    When good may have as well as bad their prime.

As when it happneth that some lovely town
Unto a barbarous besieger falls,
Who there by sword and flame himself installs
And, cruel, it in tears and blood doth drown;
Her beauty spoiled, her citizens made thralls,
His spite yet so cannot her all throw down,
But that some statue, arch, fane of renown,
Yet lurks unmaimed within her weeping walls:
So, after all the spoil, disgrace, and wrack,
That time, the world, and death could bring combined,
Amidst that mass of ruins they did make,
Safe and all scarless yet remains my mind.
    From this so high transcending rapture springs
    That I, all else defaced, not envy kings.

Ye who with curious words and Daedal's art
Frame labyrinths our beauty to surprise,
Telling strange castles forgèd in the skies,
And tales of Cupid's bow, and Cupid's dart;
Well howsoe'er ye act your feignèd smart,
Molesting quiet ears with tragic cries,
When ye accuse our chastity's best part,
Called Cruelty, ye seem not half too wise.
Even ye yourselves esteem it worthy praise,
Beauty's best guard, that Dragon which doth keep
Th' Hesperian fruit, and which in you doth raise
That Delian wit which otherwise should sleep:
    To cruel nymphs your lines do fame afford,
    Of many pitiful scarce half a word.

Fairest, when by the rules of palmistry
You took my hand to try if you could guess,
By lines therein, if any wight there be
Ordained to make me know some happiness;
I wished that those characters could explain,
Whom I will never wrong with hope to win;
Or that by them a copy might be seen,
By you, O love, what thoughts I had within.
But since the hand of Nature did not set
(As providently loth to have it known)
The means to find that hidden alphabet,
Mine eyes shall be th'interpreters alone;
 By them conceive my thoughts, and tell me, fair,
 If now you see her that doth love me there?

ROBERT HERRICK

The Argument of his Book

I sing of brooks, of blossoms, birds, and bowers:
Of April, May, of June, and July-flowers.
I sing of maypoles, hock-carts, wassails, wakes,
Of bridegrooms, brides, and of their bridal-cakes.
I write of youth, of love, and have access
By these, to sing of wantonness.
I sing of dews, of rains, and piece by piece
Of balm, of oil, of spice, and ambergris.
I sing of Time's trans-shifting; and I write
How roses first came red, and lilies white.
I sing of groves, of twilights, and I sing
The court of Mab, and of the fairy-king.
I write of Hell; I sing (and ever shall)
Of Heaven, and hope to have it after all.

Sin

Lord, with what care hast Thou begirt us round!
    Parents first season us; then schoolmasters
Deliver us to laws; they send us, bound
    To rules of reason, holy messengers,
Pulpits and Sundays, sorrow dogging sin,
    Afflictions sorted, anguish of all sizes,
Fine nets and stratagems to catch us in,
    Bibles laid open, millions of surprises;
Blessings beforehand, ties of gratefulness,
    The sound of glory ringing in our ears,
Without, our shame; within, our consciences;
    Angels and grace, eternal hopes and fears.
Yet all these fences and their whole array
One cunning bosom-sin blows quite away.

Prayer

Prayer, the Church's banquet, angels' age,
    God's breath in man returning to his birth,
The soul in paraphrase, heart in pilgrimage,
    The Christian plummet sounding heaven and earth;
Engine against the Almighty, sinner's tower,
    Reversèd thunder, Christ-side-piercing spear,
The six-days-world transposing in an hour,
    A kind of tune which all things hear and fear;
Softness, and peace, and joy, and love, and bliss,
    Exalted manna, gladness of the best,
Heaven in ordinary, man well drest,
    The milky way, the bird of paradise,
Church-bells beyond the stars heard, the soul's blood,
The land of spices, something understood.

GEORGE HERBERT

Avarice

Money, thou bane of bliss and source of woe,
    Whence com'st thou, that thou art so fresh and fine?
I know thy parentage is base and low,—
    Man found thee poor and dirty in a mine.
Surely thou didst so little contribute
    To this great kingdom, which thou now hast got,
That he was fain, when thou wert destitute,
    To dig thee out of thy dark cave and grot.
Then forcing thee, by fire he made thee bright:
    Nay, thou hast got the face of man; for we
Have with our stamp and seal transferred our right;
    Thou art the man, and man but dross to thee.
Man calleth thee his wealth, who made thee rich;
And while he digs out thee, falls in the ditch.

WILLIAM HABINGTON

To the Moment Last Past

O whither dost thou fly? Cannot my vow
Intreat thee tarry? Thou wert here but now,
And art thou gone? like ships that plough the sea,
And leave no print for man to track their way.
O unseen wealth! who thee did husband, can
Outvie the jewels of the ocean,
The mines of the earth! One sigh well spent in thee
Had been a purchase for eternity!
We will not lose thee then. Castara, where
Shall we find out his hidden sepulchre;
And we'll revive him. Not the cruel stealth
Of fate shall rob us of so great a wealth;
    Undone in thrift! while we besought his stay,
    Ten of his fellow moments fled away.

A Rose

Blown in the morning, thou shalt fade ere noon.
What boots a life which in such haste forsakes thee?
Thou'rt wondrous frolic, being to die so soon,
And passing proud a little colour makes thee.

If thee thy brittle beauty so deceives,
Know then the thing that swells thee is thy bane;
For the same beauty doth, in bloody leaves,
The sentence of this early death contain.

Some clown's coarse lungs will poison thy sweet flower
Or by the careless plough thou shalt be torn;
And many Herods lie in wait each hour
To murder thee as soon as thou art born—

Nay, force thy bud to blow—their tyrant breath
Anticipating life, to hasten death.

JOHN MILTON

O nightingale, that on yon bloomy spray
   Warbl'st at eve, when all the woods are still,
   Thou with fresh hope the lover's heart dost fill
   While the jolly hours lead on propitious May.
Thy liquid notes that close the eye of day,
   First heard before the shallow cuckoo's bill,
   Portend success in love; O if Jove's will
   Have linkt that amorous power to thy soft lay,
Now timely sing, ere the rude bird of hate
   Foretell my hopeless doom in some grove nigh:
   As thou from year to year hast sung too late
For my relief; yet hadst no reason why,
   Whether the Muse, or Love call thee his mate,
   Both them I serve, and of their train am I.

How soon hath Time, the subtle thief of youth,
    Stol'n on his wing my three and twentieth year!
    My hasting days fly on with full career,
    But my late spring no bud or blossom show'th.
Perhaps my semblance might deceive the truth,
    That I to manhood am arrived so near,
    And inward ripeness doth much less appear,
    That some more timely-happy spirits indu'th.
Yet be it less or more, or soon or slow,
    It shall be still in strictest measure ev'n,
    To that same lot, however mean, or high,
Toward which Time leads me, and the will of Heav'n;
    All is, if I have grace to use it so,
    As ever in my great task-master's eye.

When the assault was intended to the city

Captain or Colonel, or Knight in Arms,
    Whose chance on these defenceless doors may seize,
    If ever deed of honour did thee please,
    Guard them, and him within protect from harms.
He can requite thee, for he knows the charms
    That call fame on such gentle acts as these,
    And he can spread thy name o'er lands and seas,
    Whatever clime the sun's bright circle warms.
Lift not thy spear against the Muse's bower,
    The great Emathian conqueror bid spare
    The house of Pindarus, when temple and tower
Went to the ground: and the repeated air
    Of sad Electra's poet had the power
    To save the Athenian walls from ruin bare.

Emathian conqueror: Alexander the Great, who is said to have spared
Pindar's house at the sack of Thebes in 333 B.C.
    Electra's poet: Euripides. The singing of a chorus from his play *Electra* is
said to have moved the Lacedaemonians from razing the city of Athens
which they had captured in 404 B.C.

To the Lady Margaret Ley

Daughter to that good Earl, once President
    Of England's Council and her Treasury,
    Who lived in both, unstained with gold or fee,
    And left them both, more in himself content,
Till the sad breaking of that Parliament
    Broke him, as that dishonest victory
    At Chæronea, fatal to liberty
    Killed with report that old man eloquent,
Though later born than to have known the days
    Wherein your Father flourisht, yet by you
    Madam, methinks I see him living yet;
So well your words his noble virtues praise,
    That all both judge you to relate them true,
    And to possess them, honoured Margaret.

Methought I saw my late espousèd Saint
    Brought to me like Alcestis from the grave,
    Whom Jove's great son to her glad husband gave,
    Rescued from death by force though pale and faint.
Mine as whom washt from spot of childbed taint,
    Purification in the old law did save,
    And such, as yet once more I trust to have
    Full sight of her in heaven without restraint,
Came vested all in white, pure as her mind:
    Her face was veiled, yet to my fancied sight,
    Love, sweetness, goodness, in her person shined
So clear, as in no face with more delight.
    But O as to embrace me she inclined
    I waked, she fled, and day brought back my night.

that good Earl: James Ley (1552-1629), Lord High Treasurer 1622, Lord President of the Council 1628, created Earl of Scarborough 1628.

that old man eloquent: Isocrates, who died after receiving the news of the Athenian defeat at Chæronea in 338 B.C.

On the late Massacre in Piedmont

Avenge O Lord thy slaughtered saints, whose bones
   Lie scattered on the Alpine mountains cold,
   Ev'n them who kept thy truth so pure of old
   When all our fathers worshipt stocks and stones,
Forget not: in thy book record their groans
   Who were thy sheep and in their antient fold
   Slain by the bloody Piedmontese that rolled
   Mother with infant down the rocks. Their moans
The vales redoubled to the hills, and they
   To Heav'n. Their martyred blood and ashes sow
   O'er all the Italian fields where still doth sway
The triple tyrant: that from these may grow
   A hundred-fold, who having learnt thy way
   Early may fly the Babylonian woe.

When I consider how my light is spent
   Ere half my days in this dark world and wide,
   And that one talent which is death to hide
   Lodged with me useless, though my soul more bent
To serve therewith my Maker, and present
   My true account, lest he returning chide,
   Doth God exact day-labour, light denied,
   I fondly ask; but patience to prevent
That murmur, soon replies, God doth not need
   Either man's work or his own gifts, who best
   Bear his mild yoke, they serve him best: his state
Is kingly. Thousands at his bidding speed
   And post o'er land and ocean without rest:
   They also serve who only stand and wait.

In 1655 the protestants in Piedmont were massacred by Charles Emanuel
II, Duke of Savoy.

Lawrence of virtuous father virtuous son,
  Now that the fields are dank, and ways are mire,
  Where shall we sometimes meet, and by the fire
  Help waste a sullen day; what may be won
From the hard season gaining: Time will run
  On smoother, till Favonius reinspire
  The frozen earth; and clothe in fresh attire
  The lily and the rose, that neither sowed nor spun.
What neat repast shall feast us, light and choice,
  Of Attic taste, with wine, whence we may rise
  To hear the lute well-touched, or artful voice
Warble immortal notes and Tuscan air?
  He who of these delights can judge, and spare
  To interpose them oft, is not unwise.

Cyriack, whose grandsire on the Royal Bench
  Of British Themis, with no mean applause
  Pronounced and in his volumes taught our laws,
  Which others at their Bar so often wrench:
To-day deep thoughts resolve with me to drench
  In mirth, that after no repenting draws;
  Let Euclid rest and Archimedes pause,
  And what the Swede intend, and what the French.
To measure life, learn thou betimes, and know
  Toward solid good what leads the nearest way;
  For other things mild Heaven a time ordains,
And disapproves that care, though wise in show,
  That with superfluous burden loads the day,
  And when God sends a cheerful hour, refrains.

Lawrence: one of the sons of Henry Lawrence, President of the Council
in 1654.   Favonius: the west wind.
  Cyriack Skinner: a friend of Milton, was grandson of Sir Edward Coke.

On the Detraction which followed upon my writing certain Treatises

I did but prompt the age to quit their clogs
  By the known rules of ancient liberty,
  When straight a barbarous noise environs me
  Of owls and cuckoos, asses, apes and dogs.
As when those hinds that were transformed to frogs
  Railed at Latona's twin-born progeny
  Which after held the sun and moon in fee.
  But this is got by casting pearl to hogs,
That bawl for freedom in their senseless mood,
  And still revolt when truth would set them free.
  Licence they mean when they cry liberty;
For who loves that, must first be wise and good;
  But from that mark how far they rove we see
  For all this waste of wealth, and loss of blood.

On the Lord General Fairfax at the siege of Colchester

Fairfax, whose name in arms through Europe rings,
  Filling each mouth with envy, or with praise,
  And all her jealous monarchs with amaze,
  And rumours loud, that daunt remotest kings,
Thy firm unshaken virtue ever brings
  Victory home, though new rebellions raise
  Their Hydra heads, and the false North displays
  Her broken league, to imp their serpent wings,
O yet a nobler task awaits thy hand;
  For what can war but endless war still breed,
  Till truth, and right, from violence be freed,
And public faith cleared from the shameful brand
  Of public fraud. In vain doth valour bleed
  While avarice and rapine share the land.

Latona: mother of Apollo and Artemis.

99

To the Lord General Cromwell, May 1652

Cromwell, our chief of men, who through a cloud
    Not of war only, but detractions rude,
    Guided by faith and matchless fortitude
    To peace and truth thy glorious way hast ploughed
And on the neck of crownèd Fortune proud
    Hast reared God's trophies, and his work pursued,
    While Darwen stream with blood of Scots imbrued,
    And Dunbar field resounds thy praises loud,
And Worcester's laureate wreath; yet much remains
    To conquer still; peace hath her victories
    No less renowned than war, new foes arise
Threatening to bind our souls with secular chains:
    Help us to save free conscience from the paw
    Of hireling wolves whose gospel is their maw.

To Mr. Cyriack Skinner upon his Blindness

Cyriack, this three years day these eyes, though clear
    To outward view, of blemish or of spot,
    Bereft of light their seeing have forgot,
    Nor to their idle orbs doth sight appear
Of sun or moon or star throughout the year,
    Or man or woman. Yet I argue not
    Against heaven's hand or will, nor bate a jot
    Of heart or hope; but still bear up and steer
Right onward. What supports me, dost thou ask?
    The conscience, Friend, to have lost them overplied
    In liberty's defence, my noble task,
Of which all Europe talks from side to side.
    This thought might lead me through the world's
        vain mask
    Content though blind, had I no better guide.

JOHN MILTON
To Sir Henry Vane the Younger

Vane, young in years but in sage counsel old,
    Than whom a better senator ne'er held
    The helm of Rome, when gowns, not arms, repelled
    The fierce Epirot and the African bold,
Whether to settle peace, or to unfold
    The drift of hollow states hard to be spelled;
    Then to advise how war may, best upheld,
    Move by her two main nerves, iron and gold,
In all her equipage; besides, to know
    Both spiritual power and civil, what each means,
    What severs each, thou'st learnt, which few have done.
The bounds of either sword to thee we owe:
    Therefore on thy firm hand Religion leans
    In peace, and reckons thee her eldest son.

SIR JOHN SUCKLING
Love Turned to Hatred

I will not love one minute more, I swear,
No, not a minute; not a sigh or tear
Thou get'st from me, or one kind look agen,
Though thou shouldst court me to't and wouldst begin.
I will not think of thee but as men do
Of debts and sins, and then I'll curse thee too:
For thy sake woman shall be now to me
Less welcome than at midnight ghosts shall be:
I'll hate so perfectly that it shall be
Treason to love that man that loves a she;
Nay, I will hate the very good, I swear,
That's in thy sex, because it doth lie there;
Their very virtue, grace, discourse, and wit,
And all for thee; what, wilt thou love me yet?

Sir Henry Vane the Younger, 1612–62, at one time Treasurer of the Navy.
Epirot: Pyrrhus, repelled in 279 B.C.   the African: Hannibal.

Two Sisters

I

Alice is tall and upright as a pine,
White as blanched almonds or the falling snow,
Sweet as are damask roses when they blow,
And doubtless fruitful as the swelling vine.
Ripe to be cut and ready to be pressed,
Her full-cheeked beauties very well appear,
And a year's fruit she loses every year,
Wanting a man to improve her to the best.
Full fain she would be husbanded, and yet,
Alas, she cannot a fit labourer get
To cultivate her to his own content:
Fain would she be, God wot, about her task,
And yet, forsooth, she is too proud to ask,
And (which is worse) too modest to consent.

II

Margaret of humbler stature by the head
Is (as it oft falls out with yellow hair)
Than her fair sister, yet so much more fair
As her pure white is better mixt with red.
This, hotter than the other ten to one,
Longs to be put unto her mother's trade,
And loud proclaims she lives too long a maid,
Wishing for one to untie her virgin zone.
She finds virginity a kind of ware
That's very, very troublesome to bear,
And being gone she thinks will ne'er be missed;
And yet withal the girl has so much grace,
To call for help I know she wants the face,
Though, asked, I know not how she would resist.

BENJAMIN STILLINGFLEET

When I behold thee, blameless Williamson,
    Wrecked like an infant on a savage shore,
    While others round on borrowed pinions soar,
My busy fancy calls thy thread misspun;
Till Faith instructs me the deceit to shun,
    While thus she speaks: Those wings that from the store
    Of virtue were not lent, howe'er they bore
In this gross air, will melt when near the sun.
The truly ambitious wait for Nature's time,
    Content by certain though by slow degrees
    To mount above the reach of vulgar flight:
Nor is that man confined to this low clime
    Who but the extremist skirts of glory sees;
    And hears celestial echoes with delight.

WILLIAM WALSH

What has this bugbear death that's worth our care?
    After a life of pain and sorrow past,
After deluding hopes and dire despair,
    Death only gives us quiet at the last;
    How strangely are our love and hate misplaced!
Freedom we seek, and yet from freedom flee,
    Courting those tyrant-sins that chain us fast,
And shunning death that only sets us free.
'Tis not a foolish fear of future pains,—
Why should they fear who keep their souls from stains?—
    That makes me dread thy terrors, Death, to see,
'Tis not the loss of riches or of fame,
Or the vain toys the vulgar pleasures name,
    'Tis nothing, Celia, but the losing thee!

THOMAS GRAY

On the Death of Richard West

In vain to me the smiling mornings shine,
　And red'ning Phoebus lifts his golden fire:
The birds in vain their amorous descant join;
　Or cheerful fields resume their green attire:
These ears, alas! for other notes repine,
　A different object do these eyes require.
My lonely anguish melts no heart but mine;
　And in my breast the imperfect joys expire.
Yet morning smiles the busy race to cheer,
　And new-born pleasure brings to happier men:
The fields to all their wonted tribute bear:
　To warm their little loves the birds complain:
I fruitless mourn to him that cannot hear,
　And weep the more because I weep in vain.

WILLIAM MASON

A plaintive sonnet flowed from Milton's pen
　When time had stol'n his three and twentieth year:
Say shall not I then shed one tuneful tear,
　Robbed by the thief of threescore years and ten?
No! for the foes of all life-lengthened men,
　Trouble and toil, approach not yet too near;
　Reason, meanwhile, and health, and memory dear
Hold unimpaired their weak, yet wonted reign:
　Still round my sheltered lawn I pleased can stray;
Still trace my sylvan blessings to their spring:
　Being of Beings! Yes, that silent lay
Which musing Gratitude delights to sing,
　Still to thy sapphire throne shall faith convey,
　And hope, the cherub of unwearied wing.

THOMAS WARTON

To the River Lodon

Ah! what a weary race my feet have run
   Since first I trod thy banks with alders crowned,
   And thought my way was all through fairy ground,
Beneath thy azure sky and golden sun:
Where first my Muse to lisp her notes begun!
   While pensive memory traces back the round
Which fills the varied interval between;
Much pleasure, more of sorrow, marks the scene.
Sweet native stream! those skies and suns so pure
   No more return, to cheer my evening road!
Yet still one joy remains,—that not obscure,
   Nor useless, all my vacant days have flowed,
From youth's gay dawn to manhood's prime mature;
   Nor with the Muse's laurel unbestowed.

From Pembroke's princely dome, where mimic art
   Decks with a magic hand the dazzling bowers,
   Its living hues where the warm pencil pours,
   And breathing forms from the rude marble start,
How to life's humbler scene can I depart?
   My breast all glowing from those gorgeous towers,
   In my low cell how cheat the sullen hours!
   Vain the complaint: for Fancy can impart
(To fate superior, and to Fortune's doom)
   Whate'er adorns the stately-storied hall:
   She, mid the dungeon's solitary gloom,
Can dress the Graces in the Attic pall:
   Bid the green landskip's vernal beauty bloom;
   And in bright trophies clothe the twilight wall.

To Mrs. Unwin

Mary! I want a lyre with other strings,
  Such aid from heaven as some have feigned they drew,
  An eloquence scarce given to mortals, new
And undebased by praise of meaner things;
That, ere through age or woe I shed my wings,
  I may record thy worth with honour due,
  In verse as musical as thou art true,
And that immortalizes whom it sings.
But thou hast little need. There is a Book
  By seraphs writ with beams of heavenly light,
On which the eyes of God not rarely look,
  A chronicle of actions just and bright;—
There all thy deeds, my faithful Mary, shine;
And since thou own'st that praise, I spare thee mine.

Spring
Wherein each thing renews save only happiness

The garlands fade that Spring so lately wove,
  Each simple flower, which she had nurst in dew,
Anemonies that spangled every grove,
  The primrose wan, and hare-bell, mildly blue.
No more shall violets linger in the dell
  Or purple orchis variegate the plain,
Till spring again shall call forth every bell,
  And dress with humid hands her wreaths again.
Ah! poor humanity! so frail, so fair,
  Are the fond visions of thy early day,
Till tyrant passion, and corrosive care,
  Bid all thy fairy colours fade away!
Another May new buds and flowers shall bring;
Ah! why has happiness no second spring?

JOHN CODRINGTON BAMPFYLDE

On a Wet Summer

All ye who far from town in rural hall,
    Like me, were wont to dwell near pleasant field,
    Enjoying all the sunny day did yield,
With me the change lament, in irksome thrall,
By rains incessant held; for now no call
    From early swain invites my hand to wield
    The scythe. In parlour dim I sit concealed,
And mark the lessening sand from hour-glass fall;
Or 'neath my window view the wistful train
    Of dripping poultry, whom the vine's broad leaves
Shelter no more. Mute is the mournful plain;
    Silent the swallow sits beneath the thatch,
    And vacant hind hangs pensive o'er his hatch,
Counting the frequent drips from reeded eaves.

THOMAS RUSSELL

Philoctetes

On this lone isle whose rugged rocks affright
    The cautious pilot, ten revolving years
    Great Pœan's son, unwonted erst to tears,
Wept o'er his wound: alike each rolling light
Of Heaven he watched, and blamed its lingering flight.
    By day the sea-mew screaming round his cave
    Drove slumber from his eyes; the chiding wave
And savage howlings chased his dreams by night.
Hope still was his: in each low breeze that sighed
    Through his rude grot, he heard a coming oar,
In each white cloud a coming sail he spied;
    Nor seldom listened to the fancied roar
Of Œta's torrents, or the hoarser tide
    That parts famed Trachis from the Euboic shore.

this lone isle: Thasos, where Philoctetes, the son of Pœas, the most
famous archer of the Greek war, was left because of a wound in his foot.
    Œta: a mountain in Thessaly on the E. Coast of Greece.

To Hope

O ever skilled to wear the form we love,
   To bid the shapes of fear and grief depart;
Come gentle Hope! with one gay smile remove
   The lasting sadness of an aching heart.
Thy voice, benign Enchantress! let me hear;
   Say that for me some pleasures yet shall bloom,
That Fancy's radiance, Friendship's precious tear,
   Shall soften, or shall chase, misfortune's gloom.
But come not glowing in the dazzling ray
   Which once with dear illusions charmed my eye,
O! strew no more, sweet flatterer! on my way
   The flowers I fondly thought too bright to die;
Visions less fair will soothe my pensive breast,
That asks not happiness, but longs for rest!

Influence of Time on Grief

O Time! who know'st a lenient hand to lay
   Softest on sorrow's wounds, and slowly thence,
   (Lulling to sad repose the weary sense)
The faint pang stealest unperceived away;
   On Thee I rest my only hope at last,
And think, when thou hast dried the bitter tear
That flows in vain o'er all my soul held dear,
   I may look back on many a sorrow past,
And meet life's peaceful evening with a smile—
   As some lone bird, at day's departing hour,
   Sings in the sunbeam, of the transient shower
Forgetful, tho' its wings are wet the while;—
   Yet ah! how much must that poor heart endure,
   Which hopes from thee, and thee alone, a cure!

WILLIAM LISLE BOWLES

Ostend
On Hearing the Bells at Sea

How sweet the tuneful bells' responsive peal!
　　As when at opening dawn the fragrant breeze
　　Touches the trembling sense of pale disease,
So piercing to my heart their force I feel.
　　And hark! with lessening cadence now they fall,
And now along the white and level tide
They fling their melancholy music wide;
　　Bidding me many a tender thought recall
Of summer days, and those delightful years
　　When by my native streams, in life's fair prime,
　　The mournful magic of their mingling chime
First waked my wondering childhood into tears!
　　But seeming now, when all those days are o'er,
　　The sound of joy once heard and heard no more.

WILLIAM WORDSWORTH

Nuns fret not at their convent's narrow room;
And hermits are contented with their cells;
And students with their pensive citadels;
Maids at the wheel, the weaver at his loom,
Sit blithe and happy; bees that soar for bloom,
High as the highest peak of Furness-fells,
Will murmur by the hour in foxglove bells:
In truth the prison, unto which we doom
Ourselves, no prison is: and hence for me,
In sundry moods, 'twas pastime to be bound
Within the sonnet's scanty plot of ground;
Pleased if some souls (for such there needs must be)
Who have felt the weight of too much liberty,
Should find brief solace there, as I have found.

A flock of sheep that leisurely pass by,
One after one; the sound of rain, and bees
Murmuring; the fall of rivers, winds and seas,
Smooth fields, white sheets of water, and pure sky;
I have thought of all by turns, and yet do lie
Sleepless! and soon the small birds' melodies
Must hear, first uttered from my orchard trees;
And the first cuckoo's melancholy cry.
Even thus last night, and two nights more, I lay
And could not win thee, Sleep! by any stealth:
So do not let me wear to-night away:
Without Thee what is all the morning's wealth?
Come, blessed barrier between day and day,
Dear mother of fresh thoughts and joyous health!

Surprised by joy—impatient as the wind
I turned to share the transport—Oh! with whom
But Thee, deep buried in the silent tomb,
That spot which no vicissitude can find?
Love, faithful love, recalled thee to my mind—
But how could I forget thee? Through what power,
Even for the least division of an hour,
Have I been so beguiled as to be blind
To my most grievous loss!—That thought's return
Was the worst pang that sorrow ever bore,
Save one, one only, when I stood forlorn,
Knowing my heart's best treasure was no more;
That neither present time, nor years unborn
Could to my sight that heavenly face restore.

It is a beauteous evening, calm and free,
The holy time is quiet as a nun
Breathless with adoration; the broad sun
Is sinking down in its tranquility;
The gentleness of heaven broods o'er the sea:
Listen! the mighty Being is awake,
And doth with his eternal motion make
A sound like thunder—everlastingly.
Dear child! dear girl! that walkest with me here,
If thou appear untouched by solemn thought,
Thy nature is not therefore less divine:
Thou liest in Abraham's bosom all the year;
And worship'st at the Temple's inner shrine,
God being with thee when we know it not.

The world is too much with us; late and soon,
Getting and spending, we lay waste our powers:
Little we see in Nature that is ours;
We have given our hearts away, a sordid boon!
The sea that bares her bosom to the moon;
The winds that will be howling at all hours,
And are up-gathered now like sleeping flowers;
For this, for everything, we are out of tune;
It moves us not.—Great God! I'd rather be
A Pagan suckled in a creed outworn;
So might I, standing on this pleasant lea,
Have glimpses that would make me less forlorn;
Have sight of Proteus rising from the sea;
Or hear old Triton blow his wreathèd horn.

Scorn not the sonnet; Critic, you have frowned,
Mindless of its just honours; with this key
Shakespeare unlocked his heart; the melody
Of this small lute gave ease to Petrarch's wound;
A thousand times this pipe did Tasso sound;
With it Camöens soothed an exile's grief;
The sonnet glittered a gay myrtle leaf
Amid the cypress with which Dante crowned
His visionary brow: a glow-worm lamp,
It cheered mild Spenser, called from faery-land
To struggle through dark ways; and when a damp
Fell round the path of Milton, in his hand
The thing became a trumpet; whence he blew
Soul-animating strains—alas, too few!

Composed upon Westminster Bridge, September 3, 1802

Earth has not anything to show more fair:
Dull would he be of soul who could pass by
A sight more touching in its majesty:
This City now doth, like a garment, wear
The beauty of the morning; silent, bare,
Ships, towers, domes, theatres, and temples lie
Open unto the fields, and to the sky;
All bright and glittering in the smokeless air.
Never did sun more beautifully steep
In his first splendour, valley, rock, or hill;
Ne'er saw I, never felt, a calm so deep!
The river glideth at his own sweet will:
Dear God! the very houses seem asleep;
And all that mighty heart is lying still!

Why art thou silent? Is thy love a plant
Of such weak fibre that the treacherous air
Of absence withers what was once so fair?
Is there no debt to pay, no boon to grant?
Yet have my thoughts for thee been vigilant—
Bound to thy service with unceasing care,
The mind's least generous wish a mendicant
For nought but what thy happiness could spare.
Speak—though this soft warm heart, once free to hold
A thousand tender pleasures, thine and mine,
Be left more desolate, more dreary cold
Than a forsaken bird's-nest filled with snow
'Mid its own bush of leafless eglantine—
Speak, that my torturing doubts their end may know!

On the Extinction of the Venetian Republic

Once did she hold the gorgeous east in fee;
And was the safeguard of the west: the worth
Of Venice did not fall below her birth,
Venice, the eldest child of Liberty.
She was a maiden city, bright and free;
No guile seduced, no force could violate;
And, when she took unto herself a mate,
She must espouse the everlasting sea.
And what if she had seen those glories fade,
Those titles vanish, and that strength decay;
Yet shall some tribute of regret be paid
When her long life hath reached its final day:
Men are we, and must grieve when even the shade
Of that which once was great is passed away.

Venice lost her independence in 1797, when Napoleon made her part
of Austria.

To Toussaint L'Ouverture

Toussaint, the most unhappy man of men!
Whether the whistling rustic tend his plough
Within thy hearing, or thy head be now
Pillowed in some deep dungeon's earless den;—
O miserable Chieftain! where and when
Wilt thou find patience! Yet die not; do thou
Wear rather in thy bonds a cheerful brow:
Though fallen thyself, never to rise again,
Live, and take comfort. Thou hast left behind
Powers that will work for thee; air, earth, and skies;
There's not a breathing of the common wind
That will forget thee; thou hast great allies;
Thy friends are exultations, agonies,
And love, and man's unconquerable mind.

Thought of a Briton on the Subjugation of Switzerland

Two Voices are there; one is of the sea,
One of the mountains; each a mighty Voice:
In both from age to age thou didst rejoice,
They were thy chosen music, Liberty!
There came a tyrant, and with holy glee
Thou fought'st against him; but hast vainly striven:
Thou from thy Alpine holds at length art driven,
Where not a torrent murmurs heard by thee.
Of one deep bliss thine ear hath been bereft:
Then cleave, O cleave to that which still is left;
For, high-souled Maid, what sorrow would it be
That mountain floods should thunder as before,
And ocean bellow from his rocky shore,
And neither awful Voice be heard by thee!

Toussaint: François Dominique Toussaint l'Ouverture (1743–1803), a San Domingo negro, ruled the island by authority from the Directory from 1796, but because he resisted Napoleon's re-introduction of slavery in 1801 was sent to France, where he died in prison.

Written in London, September, 1802

O Friend! I know not which way I must look
For comfort, being, as I am, opprest,
To think that now our life is only drest
For show; mean handiwork of craftsman, cook,
Or groom!—We must run glittering like a brook
In the open sunshine, or we are unblest:
The wealthiest man among us is the best:
No grandeur now in nature or in book
Delights us. Rapine, avarice, expense,
This is idolatry; and these we adore:
Plain living and high thinking are no more:
The homely beauty of the good old cause
Is gone; our peace, our fearful innocence,
And pure religion breathing household laws.

London, 1802

Milton! thou shouldst be living at this hour:
England hath need of thee: she is a fen
Of stagnant waters: altar, sword, and pen,
Fireside, the heroic wealth of hall and bower,
Have forfeited their ancient English dower
Of inward happiness. We are selfish men;
Oh! raise us up, return to us again;
And give us manners, virtue, freedom, power.
Thy soul was like a star, and dwelt apart;
Thou hadst a voice whose sound was like the sea:
Pure as the naked heavens, majestic, free,
So didst thou travel on life's common way,
In cheerful godliness; and yet thy heart
The lowliest duties on herself did lay.

The River Duddon

I thought of Thee, my partner and my guide,
As being past away.—Vain sympathies!
For backward, Duddon! as I cast my eyes,
I see what was, and is, and will abide;
Still glides the stream, and shall for ever glide;
The Form remains, the Function never dies;
While we, the brave, the mighty, and the wise,
We Men, who in our morn of youth defied
The elements, must vanish;—be it so!
Enough, if something from our hands have power
To live, and act, and serve the future hour;
And if, as toward the silent tomb we go,
Through love, through hope, and faith's transcendent
    dower,
We feel that we are greater than we know.

Inside of King's College Chapel, Cambridge

Tax not the royal Saint with vain expense,
With ill-matched aims the architect who planned—
Albeit labouring for a scanty band
Of white-robed scholars only—this immense
And glorious work of fine intelligence!
Give all thou canst; high Heaven rejects the lore
Of nicely-calculated less or more;
So deemed the man who fashioned for the sense
These lofty pillars, spread that branching roof
Self-poised, and scooped into ten thousand cells,
Where light and shade repose, where music dwells
Lingering—and wandering on as loth to die;
Like thoughts whose very sweetness yieldeth proof
That they were born for immortality.

the royal Saint: King Henry VI, who founded King's College, Cam-
bridge, in 1441.

Most sweet it is with unuplifted eyes
To pace the ground, if path there be or none,
While a fair region round the traveller lies
Which he forbears again to look upon;
Pleased rather with some soft ideal scene,
The work of Fancy, or some happy tone
Of meditation, slipping in between
The beauty coming and the beauty gone.
If Thought and Love desert us, from that day
Let us break off all commerce with the Muse:
With Thought and Love companions of our way,
Whate'er the senses take or may refuse,
The mind's internal heaven shall shed her dews
Of inspiration on the humblest lay.

Mutability

From low to high doth dissolution climb,
And sink from high to low, along a scale
Of awful notes, whose concord shall not fail;
A musical but melancholy chime,
Which they can hear who meddle not with crime,
Nor avarice, nor over-anxious care.
Truth fails not; but her outward forms that bear
The longest date do melt like frosty rime,
That in the morning whitened hill and plain
And is no more; drop like the tower sublime
Of yesterday, which royally did wear
His crown of weeds, but could not even sustain
Some casual shout that broke the silent air,
Or the unimaginable touch of time.

To the Autumnal Moon

Mild splendour of the various-vested Night!
   Mother of wildly-working visions! hail!
I watch thy gliding, while with watery light
   Thy weak eye glimmers through a fleecy veil;
And when thou lovest thy pale orb to shroud
   Behind the gathered blackness lost on high;
And when thou dartest from the wind-rent cloud
   Thy placid lightning o'er the awakened sky.

Ah such is Hope! as changeful and as fair!
   Now dimly peering on the wistful sight;
Now hid behind the dragon-winged Despair:
   But soon emerging in her radiant might
She o'er the sorrow-clouded breast of care
   Sails, like a meteor kindling in its flight.

Pain

Once could the morn's first beams, the healthful breeze,
All nature, charm; and gay was every hour:—
But ah! not music's self, nor fragrant bower
Can glad the trembling sense of wan disease.
Now that the frequent pangs my frame assail,
Now that my sleepless eyes are sunk and dim,
And seas of pain seem waving through each limb—
Ah what can all life's gilded scenes avail?
I view the crowd, whom youth and health inspire,
Hear the loud laugh, and catch the sportive lay,
Then sigh and think—I too could laugh and play
And gaily sport it on the Muse's lyre,
Ere Tyrant Pain had chased away delight,
Ere the wild pulse throbbed anguish through the night!

To the River Otter

Dear native brook! wild streamlet of the West!
   How many various-fated years have past,
   What happy and what mournful hours, since last
I skimmed the smooth thin stone along thy breast,
Numbering its light leaps! yet so deep imprest
Sink the sweet scenes of childhood, that mine eyes
   I never shut amid the sunny ray,
But straight with all their tints thy waters rise,
   Thy crossing plank, thy marge with willows grey,
And bedded sand that veined with various dyes
Gleamed through thy bright transparence! On my way,
   Visions of childhood! oft have ye beguiled
Lone manhood's cares, yet waking fondest sighs:
   Ah! that once more I were a careless child!

La Fayette

As when far off the warbled strains are heard
   That soar on morning's wing the vales among;
   Within his cage the imprisoned matin bird
Swells the full chorus with a generous song:

He bathes no pinion in the dewy light,
   No father's joy, no lover's bliss he shares,
   Yet still the rising radiance cheers his sight—
His fellows' freedom soothes the captive's cares!

Thou, Fayette! who didst wake with startling voice
   Life's better sun from that long wintry night,
   Thus in thy country's triumphs shalt rejoice
And mock with raptures high the dungeon's might:

For lo! the morning struggles into day,
And slavery's spectres shriek and vanish from the ray!

To Nature

It may indeed be phantasy, when I
    Essay to draw from all created things
    Deep, heartfelt, inward joy that closely clings;
And trace in leaves and flowers that round me lie
Lessons of love and earnest piety.
    So let it be; and if the wide world rings
    In mock of this belief, it brings
Nor fear, nor grief, nor vain perplexity.
So will I build my altar in the fields,
    And the blue sky my fretted dome shall be,
And the sweet fragrance that the wild flower yields
    Shall be the incense I will yield to Thee,
Thee only God! and thou shalt not despise
Even me, the priest of this poor sacrifice.

Fancy in Nubibus
or the Poet in the Clouds

O! it is pleasant, with a heart at ease,
    Just after sunset, or by moonlight skies,
To make the shifting clouds be what you please,
    Or let the easily persuaded eyes
Own each quaint likeness issuing from the mould
    Of a friend's fancy; or with head bent low
And cheek aslant see rivers flow of gold
    'Twixt crimson banks; and then, a traveller, go
From mount to mount through Cloudland, gorgeous land!
    Or listening to the tide, with closèd sight,
Be that blind bard, who on the Chian strand
    By those deep sounds possessed with inward light,
Beheld the Iliad and the Odyssey
    Rise to the swelling of the voiceful sea.

Winter

A wrinkled crabbèd man they picture thee,
Old Winter, with a rugged beard as grey
As the long moss upon the apple-tree;
Blue-lipt, an ice-drop at thy sharp blue nose,
Close muffled up, and on thy dreary way
Plodding alone through sleet and drifting snows.
They should have drawn thee by the high-heapt hearth,
Old Winter, seated in the great armed chair,
Watching the children at their Christmas mirth;
Or circled by them as thy lips declare
Some merry jest, or tale of murder dire,
Or troubled spirit that disturbs the night,
Pausing at times to rouse the mouldering fire,
Or taste the old October brown and bright.

Corston

As thus I stand beside the murmuring stream
And watch its current, memory here pourtrays
Scenes faintly formed of half-forgotten days,
Like far-off woodlands by the moon's bright beam
Dimly descried, but lovely. I have worn
Amid these haunts the heavy hours away,
When childhood idled through the Sabbath-day;
Risen to my tasks at winter's earliest morn;
And when the summer twilight darkened here,
Thinking of home, and all of heart forlorn,
Have sighed and shed in secret many a tear.
Dreamlike and indistinct those days appear,
As the faint sounds of this low brooklet, borne
Upon the breeze, reach fitfully the ear.

Work

Who first invented work, and bound the free
And holiday-rejoicing spirit down
To the ever-haunting importunity
Of business in the green fields, and the town—
To plough, loom, anvil, spade—and oh! most sad,
To that dry drudgery at the desk's dead wood?
Who but the Being unblest, alien from good,
Sabbathless Satan! he who his unglad
Task ever plies 'mid rotatory burnings,
That round and round incalculably reel—
For wrath divine hath made him like a wheel—
In that red realm from which are no returnings;
Where toiling, and turmoiling, ever and aye
He, and his thoughts, keep pensive working-day.

JOSEPH BLANCO WHITE

Night and Death

Mysterious Night! when our first parent knew
    Thee from report divine, and heard thy name,
    Did he not tremble for this lovely frame,
This glorious canopy of light and blue?
Yet 'neath a curtain of translucent dew,
    Bathed in the rays of the great setting flame,
    Hesperus with the host of heaven came,
And lo! creation widened in man's view.
Who could have thought such darkness lay concealed
    Within thy beams, O Sun! or who could find,
Whilst fly and leaf and insect stood revealed,
    That to such countless orbs thou mad'st us blind!
        Why do we then shun death with anxious strife?
        If light can thus deceive, wherefore not life?

The springs of life are failing one by one,
  And Age with quickened step is drawing nigh;
  Yet would I heave no discontented sigh,
Since cause for cold ingratitude is none.
If slower through my veins life's tide may run,
  The heart's young fountains are not wholly dry;
  Though evening clouds shadow my noontide sky,
Night cannot quench the spirit's inward sun!
Once more then, ere the eternal bourn be passed,
  Would I my lyre's rude melody essay;
  And, while amid the chords my fingers stray,
Should Fancy sigh—'These strains may be its last!'
Yet shall not this my mind with gloom o'ercast,
  If my day's work be finished with the day!

LEIGH HUNT

The Poets

Were I to name, out of the times gone by,
  The poets dearest to me, I should say,
  Pulci for spirits, and a fine, free way;
Chaucer for manners, and close, silent eye;
Milton for classic taste, and harp strung high;
  Spenser for luxury, and sweet, sylvan play;
  Horace for chatting with, from day to day;
Shakespeare for all, but most, society.

But which to take with me, could I take but one?
  Shakespeare,—as long as I was unoppressed
    With the world's weight, making sad thoughts
        intenser;
But did I wish, out of the common sun,
  To lay a wounded heart in leafy rest,
    And dream of things far off and healing,—Spenser.

To the Grasshopper and the Cricket

Green little vaulter in the sunny grass,
    Catching your heart up at the feel of June,
    Sole voice that's heard amidst the lazy noon,
When ev'n the bees lag at the summoning brass;—
And you, warm little housekeeper, who class
    With those who think the candles come too soon,
    Loving the fire, and with your tricksome tune
Nick the glad silent moments as they pass;—

Oh sweet and tiny cousins, that belong,
    One to the fields, the other to the hearth,
Both have your sunshine; both, though small, are strong
    At your clear hearts; and both were sent on earth
To sing in thoughtful ears this natural song—
    In doors and out,—summer and winter,—Mirth.

The Nile

It flows through all hushed Egypt and its sands
    Like some grave mighty thought threading a dream,
    And time and things, as in that vision, seem
Keeping along it their eternal stands,—
Caves, pillars, pyramids, the shepherd bands
    That roamed through the young world, the glory extreme
    Of high Sesostris, and that southern beam,
The laughing queen that caught the world's great hands.
Then comes a mightier silence, stern and strong,
As of a world left empty of its throng,
    And the void weighs on us; and then we wake,
And hear the fruitful stream lapsing along
    'Twixt villages, and think how we shall take
    Our own calm journey on for human sake.

The Fish, the Man, and the Spirit
To a Fish

You strange, astonished-looking, angle-faced,
  Dreary-mouthed, gaping wretches of the sea,
  Gulping salt-water everlastingly,
Cold-blooded, though with red your blood be graced,
And mute, though dwellers in the roaring waste;
  And you, all shapes beside, that fishy be,—
  Some round, some flat, some long, all devilry,
Legless, unloving, infamously chaste:—

O scaly, slippery, wet, swift, staring wights,
  What is't ye do? What life lead? eh, dull goggles?
How do ye vary your vile days and nights?
  How pass your Sundays? Are ye still but joggles
In ceaseless wash? Still nought but gapes, and bites,
  And drinks, and stares, diversified with boggles?

A Fish Answers

Amazing monster! that, for aught I know,
  With the first sight of thee didst make our race
  For ever stare! O flat and shocking face,
Grimly divided from the breast below!
Thou that on dry land horribly dost go
  With a split body and most ridiculous pace,
  Prong after prong, disgracer of all grace,
Long-useless-finned, haired, upright, unwet, slow!

O breather of unbreathable, sharp-sword air,
  How canst exist? How bear thyself, thou dry
And dreary sloth? What particle canst share
  Of the only blessed life, the watery?
I sometimes see of ye an actual *pair*
  Go by! linked fin by fin! most odiously.

The Fish Turns into a Man, and then into a Spirit, and again Speaks

Indulge thy smiling scorn, if smiling still,
    O man! and loathe, but with a sort of love;
    For difference must its use by difference prove,
And, in sweet clang, the spheres with music fill.
One of the spirits am I, that at his will
    Live in whate'er has life—fish, eagle, dove—
    No hate, no pride, beneath nought, nor above,
A visitor of the rounds of God's sweet skill.

Man's life is warm, glad, sad, 'twixt loves and graves,
    Boundless in hope, honoured with pangs austere,
Heaven-gazing; and his angel-wings he craves:—
    The fish is swift, small-needing, vague yet clear,
A cold, sweet, silver life, wrapped in round waves,
    Quickened with touches of transporting fear.

SIR AUBREY DE VERE

The 'Children's Crusade'

All holy influences dwell within
    The breast of Childhood: instincts fresh from God
    Inspire it, ere the heart beneath the rod
Of grief hath bled, or caught the plague of sin.
How mighty was that fervour which could win
    Its way to infant souls!—and was the sod
    Of Palestine by infant Croises trod?
Like Joseph went they forth, or Benjamin,
In all their touching beauty, to redeem?
    And did their soft lips kiss the sepulchre?
Alas! the lovely pageant, as a dream,
    Faded! they sank not through ignoble fear;
They felt not Moslem steel. By mountain, stream,
    In sands, in fens, they died—no mother near!

GEORGE GORDON, LORD BYRON
On Chillon

Eternal Spirit of the chainless Mind!
    Brightest in dungeons, Liberty, thou art—
    For there thy habitation is the heart—
The heart which love of thee alone can bind;
And when thy sons to fetters are consigned,
    To fetters, and the damp vault's dayless gloom,
    Their country conquers with their martyrdom,
And Freedom's fame finds wings on every wind.
Chillon! thy prison is a holy place,
    And thy sad floor an altar, for 'twas trod,
Until his very steps have left a trace
    Worn as if thy cold pavement were a sod,
By Bonnivard! May none those marks efface!
    For they appeal from tyranny to God.

PERCY BYSSHE SHELLEY
Ozymandias

I met a traveller from an antique land
Who said: Two vast and trunkless legs of stone
Stand in the desert ... Near them, on the sand,
Half sunk, a shattered visage lies, whose frown,
And wrinkled lip, and sneer of cold command,
Tell that the sculptor well those passions read
Which yet survive, stamped on these lifeless things,
The hand that mocked them, and the heart that fed;
And on the pedestal these words appear:
'My name is Ozymandias, king of kings:
Look on my works, ye Mighty, and despair!'
Nothing beside remains. Round the decay
Of that colossal wreck, boundless and bare
The lone and level sands stretch far away.

Bonnivard: François de Bonnivard (1496- c. 1570) was imprisoned by the Duke of Savoy in the castle of Chillon, 1530-36, for attempting to set up an independent republic at Geneva.

Ye hasten to the grave! What seek ye there,
Ye restless thoughts and busy purposes
Of the idle brain, which the world's livery wear?
Oh thou quick heart, which pantest to possess
All that pale Expectation feigneth fair!
Thou vainly curious mind which wouldest guess
Whence thou didst come, and whither thou must go,
And all that never yet was known wouldst know—
Oh, whither hasten ye, that thus ye press,
With such swift feet life's green and pleasant path,
Seeking, alike from happiness and woe,
A refuge in the cavern of gray death?
O heart, and mind, and thoughts! what thing do you
Hope to inherit in the grave below?

JOHN KEATS

On First Looking into Chapman's Homer

Much have I travelled in the realms of gold,
    And many goodly states and kingdoms seen;
    Round many western islands have I been
Which bards in fealty to Apollo hold.
Oft of one wide expanse had I been told
    That deep-browed Homer ruled as his demesne;
    Yet did I never breathe its pure serene
Till I heard Chapman speak out loud and bold.
Then felt I like some watcher of the skies
    When a new planet swims into his ken;
Or like stout Cortez when with eagle eyes
    He stared at the Pacific—and all his men
Looked at each other with a wild surmise—
    Silent, upon a peak in Darien.

To Homer

Standing aloof in giant ignorance,
    Of thee I hear and of the Cyclades,
As one who sits ashore and longs perchance
    To visit dolphin-coral in deep seas.
So thou wast blind!—but then the veil was rent,
    For Jove uncurtained Heaven to let thee live,
And Neptune made for thee a spumy tent,
    And Pan made sing for thee his forest-hive;
Aye, on the shores of darkness there is light,
    And precipices show untrodden green;
There is a budding morrow in midnight;
    There is a triple sight in blindness keen;
Such seeing hadst thou, as it once befel
To Dian, Queen of Earth, and Heaven, and Hell.

To Sleep

O soft embalmer of the still midnight,
    Shutting, with careful fingers and benign,
Our gloom-pleased eyes, embowered from the
    light,
    Enshaded in forgetfulness divine;
O soothest Sleep! if so it please thee, close,
    In midst of this thine hymn, my willing eyes,
Or wait the amen, ere thy poppy throws
    Around my bed its lulling charities;
    Then save me, or the passèd day will shine
Upon my pillow, breeding many woes;
    Save me from curious conscience, that still lords
Its strength for darkness, burrowing like a mole;
    Turn the key deftly in the oilèd wards,
And seal the hushèd casket of my soul.

Oh! how I love, on a fair summer's eve,
When streams of light pour down the golden
west,
And on the balmy zephyrs tranquil rest
The silver clouds, far—far away to leave
All meaner thoughts, and take a sweet reprieve
From little cares; to find, with quiet quest,
A fragrant wild, with Nature's beauty drest,
And there into delight my soul deceive.
There warm my breast with patriotic lore,
Musing on Milton's fate—on Sidney's bier—
Till their stern forms before my mind arise:
Perhaps on the wing of Poesy upsoar,
Full often dropping a delicious tear,
When some melodious sorrow spells mine eye.

After dark vapours have oppressed our plains
For a long dreary season, comes a day
Born of the gentle South, and clears away
From the sick heavens all unseemly stains.
The anxious month, relieving from its pains,
Takes as a long-lost right the feel of May,
The eyelids with the passing coolness play,
Like rose leaves with the drip of summer rains.
The calmest thoughts come round us—as of leaves
Budding,—fruit ripening in stillness,—autumn suns
Smiling at eve upon the quiet sheaves,—
Sweet Sappho's cheek,—a sleeping infant's breath,—
The gradual sand that through an hour-glass runs,—
A woodland rivulet,—a Poet's death.

On the Sea

It keeps eternal whisperings around
   Desolate shores, and with its mighty swell
   Gluts twice ten thousand caverns, till the spell
Of Hecate leaves them their old shadowy sound.
Often 'tis in such gentle temper found,
   That scarcely will the very smallest shell
   Be moved for days from where it sometime fell,
When last the winds of heaven were unbound.
Oh ye! who have your eye-balls vexed and tired,
   Feast them upon the wideness of the Sea;
      Oh ye! whose ears are dinned with uproar rude,
   Or fed too much with cloying melody,—
      Sit ye near some old cavern's mouth, and brood
   Until ye start, as if the sea-nymphs quired!

When I have fears that I may cease to be
   Before my pen has gleaned my teeming brain,
Before high-pilèd books, in charact'ry,
   Hold like rich garners the full-ripened grain;
When I behold, upon the night's starred face,
   Huge cloudy symbols of a high romance,
And think that I may never live to trace
   Their shadows, with the magic hand of chance;
And when I feel, fair creature of an hour!
   That I shall never look upon thee more,
Never have relish in the faery power
   Of unreflecting love!—then on the shore
Of the wide world I stand alone, and think
Till love and fame to nothingness do sink.

Answer to a Sonnet ending thus:—

> '*Dark eyes are dearer far*
> *Than those that mock the hyacinthine bell;*'
> By *J. H. Reynolds.*

Blue! 'Tis the life of heaven,—the domain
   Of Cynthia,—the wide palace of the sun,—
The tent of Hesperus, and all his train,—
   The bosomer of clouds, gold, grey and dun.
Blue! 'Tis the life of waters—ocean
   And all its vassal streams: pools numberless
May rage, and foam, and fret, but never can
   Subside, if not to dark-blue nativeness.
Blue! Gentle cousin of the forest-green,
   Married to green in all the sweetest flowers,—
Forget-me-not,—the blue bell,—and, that queen
   Of secrecy, the violet: what strange powers
Hast thou, as a mere shadow! But how great,
When in an Eye thou art alive with fate!

On Fame

Fame, like a wayward girl, will still be coy
   To those who woo her with too slavish knees,
But makes surrender to some thoughtless boy,
   And dotes the more upon a heart at ease;
She is a Gipsy, will not speak to those
   Who have not learnt to be content without her;
A Jilt, whose ear was never whispered close,
   Who thinks they scandal her who talk about her;
A very Gipsy is she, Nilus-born,
   Sister-in-law to jealous Potiphar;
Ye love-sick Bards! repay her scorn for scorn;
   Ye Artists lovelorn! madmen that ye are!
Make your best bow to her and bid adieu,
Then, if she likes it, she will follow you.

On Fame

'You cannot eat your cake and have it too,'—*Proverb.*

How fevered is the man who cannot look
   Upon his mortal days with temperate blood,
Who vexes all the leaves of his life's book,
   And robs his fair name of its maidenhood;
It is as if the rose should pluck herself,
   Or the ripe plum finger its misty bloom,
As if a Naiad, like a meddling elf,
   Should darken her pure grot with muddy gloom:
But the rose leaves herself upon the briar,
   For winds to kiss and grateful bees to feed,
And the ripe plum still wears its dim attire,
   The undisturbèd lake has crystal space;
   Why then should man, teasing the world for grace,
Spoil his salvation for a fierce miscreed?

If by dull rhymes our English must be chained,
And, like Andromeda, the Sonnet sweet
Fettered, in spite of painèd loveliness;
   Let us find out, if we must be constrained,
Sandals more interwoven and complete
To fit the naked foot of poesy:
   Let us inspect the lyre, and weigh the stress
Of every chord, and see what may be gained
By ear industrious, and attention meet;
Misers of sound and syllable, no less
Than Midas of his coinage, let us be
Jealous of dead leaves in the bay wreath crown;
So, if we may not let the Muse be free,
She will be bound with garlands of her own.

To Ailsa Rock

Hearken, thou craggy ocean pyramid!
    Give answer from thy voice, the sea-fowls' screams!
    When were thy shoulders mantled in huge streams?
When from the sun was thy broad forehead hid?
How long since is't since the mighty Power bid
    Thee heave to airy sleep from fathom dreams?
    Sleep in the lap of thunder or sunbeams,
Or when grey clouds are thy cold coverlid.
Thou answer'st not; for thou art dead asleep;
    Thy life is but two dead eternities—
The last in air, the former in the deep;
    First with the whales, last with the eagle-skies—
Drownèd wast thou till an earthquake made thee steep,
    Another cannot wake thy giant size.

Four seasons fill the measure of the year;
    There are four seasons in the mind of man:
He has his lusty Spring, when fancy clear
    Takes in all beauty with an easy span:
He has his Summer, when luxuriously
    Spring's honied cud of youthful thought he loves
To ruminate, and by such dreaming nigh
    His nearest unto heaven: quiet coves
His soul has in its Autumn, when his wings
    He furleth close; contented so to look
On mists in idleness—to let fair things
    Pass by unheeded as a threshold brook.
He has his Winter too of pale misfeature,
Or else he would forego his mortal nature.

To one who has been long in city pent,
   'Tis very sweet to look into the fair
   And open face of heaven,—to breathe a prayer
Full in the smile of the blue firmament.
Who is more happy, when, with heart's content,
   Fatigued he sinks into some pleasant lair
   Of wavy grass, and reads a debonair
And gentle tale of love and languishment?
Returning home at evening, with an ear
   Catching the notes of Philomel,—an eye
Watching the sailing cloudlet's bright career,
   He mourns that day so soon has glided by:
E'en like the passage of an angel's tear
   That falls through the clear ether silently.

Bright star! would I were steadfast as thou art—
   Not in lone splendour hung aloft the night
And watching, with eternal lids apart,
   Like nature's patient, sleepless Eremite,
The moving waters at their priestlike task
   Of pure ablution round earth's human shores,
Or gazing on the new soft fallen mask
   Of snow upon the mountains and the moors—
No—yet still steadfast, still unchangeable,
   Pillowed upon my fair love's ripening breast,
To feel for ever its soft fall and swell,
   Awake for ever in a sweet unrest,
Still, still to hear her tender-taken breath,
And so live ever—or else swoon to death.

Prayer

Be not afraid to pray—to pray is right.
  Pray, if thou canst, with hope; but ever pray,
  Though hope be weak, or sick with long delay;
Pray in the darkness, if there be no light.
Far is the time, remote from human sight,
  When war and discord on the earth shall cease;
  Yet every prayer for universal peace
Avails the blessed time to expedite.
Whate'er is good to wish, ask that of Heaven,
  Though it be what thou canst not hope to see:
Pray to be perfect, though material leaven
  Forbid the spirit so on earth to be;
But if for any wish thou darest not pray,
Then pray to God to cast that wish away.

To a Friend

When we were idlers with the loitering rills,
  The need of human love we little noted:
  Our love was nature; and the peace that floated
On the white mist, and dwelt upon the hills,
To sweet accord subdued our wayward wills:
  One soul was ours, one mind, one heart devoted,
  That, wisely doting, asked not why it doted,
And ours the unknown joy, which knowing kills.
But now I find how dear thou wert to me;
  That man is more than half of nature's treasure,
Of that fair beauty which no eye can see,
  Of that sweet music which no ear can measure;
  And now the streams may sing for others' pleasure,
The hills sleep on in their eternity.

September

The dark green summer, with its massive hues,
    Fades into autumn's tincture manifold;
    A gorgeous garniture of fire and gold
The high slope of the ferny hills indues;
The mists of morn in slumbering layers diffuse
    O'er glimmering rock, smooth lake, and spiked array
    Of hedgerow thorns, a unity of gray;
All things appear their tangible form to lose
In ghostly vastness. But anon the gloom
    Melts, as the sun puts off his muddy veil;
And now the birds their twittering songs resume,
    All summer silent in the leafy dale.
In spring they piped of love on every tree,
But now they sing the song of memory.

To a Lofty Beauty, from her Poor Kinsman

Fair maid, had I not heard thy baby cries,
    Nor seen thy girlish, sweet vicissitude,
    Thy mazy motions, striving to elude,
Yet wooing still a parent's watchful eyes,
Thy humours, many as the opal's dyes,
    And lovely all;—methinks thy scornful mood,
    And bearing high of stately womanhood,—
Thy brow, where Beauty sits to tyrannize
    O'er humble love, had made me sadly fear thee;
For never sure was seen a royal bride
Whose gentleness gave grace to so much pride—
    My very thoughts would tremble to be near thee:
But when I see thee at thy father's side,
    Old times unqueen thee, and old loves endear thee.

May, 1840

A lovely morn, so still, so very still,
   It hardly seems a growing day of Spring,
   Though all the odorous buds are blossoming,
And the small matin birds were glad and shrill
Some hours ago; but now the woodland rill
   Murmurs along, the only vocal thing,
   Save when the wee wren flits with stealthy wing,
And cons by fits and bits her evening trill.
Lovers might sit on such a morn as this
   An hour together, looking at the sky,
Nor dare to break the silence with a kiss,
   Long listening for the signal of a sigh;
And the sweet Nun, diffused in voiceless prayer,
Feed her own soul through all the brooding air.

November

The mellow year is hasting to its close;
The little birds have almost sung their last,
Their small notes twitter in the dreary blast—
That shrill-piped harbinger of early snows:
The patient beauty of the scentless rose,
Oft with the morn's hoar crystal quaintly glassed,
Hangs, a pale mourner for the summer past,
And makes a little summer where it grows:
In the chill sunbeam of the faint brief day
The dusky waters shudder as they shine,
The russet leaves obstruct the straggling way
Of oozy brooks, which no deep banks define,
And the gaunt woods, in ragged, scant array,
Wrap their old limbs with sombre ivy twine.

Silence

There is a silence where hath been no sound;
　　There is a silence where no sound may be,
　　In the cold grave—under the deep, deep sea,
Or in wide desert where no life is found,
Which hath been mute, and still must sleep profound;
　　No voice is hushed—no life treads silently,
　　But clouds and cloudy shadows wander free
That never spoke, over the idle ground.
But in green ruins, in the desolate walls
　　Of antique palaces, where Man hath been,
Though the dun fox, or wild hyæna, calls,
　　And owls, that flit continually between,
Shriek to the echo, and the low winds moan,
There the true Silence is, self-conscious and alone.

Death

It is not death, that sometime in a sigh
　　This eloquent breath shall take its speechless flight;
That sometime these bright stars, that now reply
　　In sunlight to the sun, shall set in night,
　　That this warm conscious flesh shall perish quite,
And all life's ruddy springs forget to flow;
　　That thoughts shall cease, and the immortal sprite
Be lapped in alien clay and laid below;
It is not death to know this,—but to know
　　That pious thoughts, which visit at new graves
In tender pilgrimage, will cease to go
　　So duly and so oft,—and when grass waves
Over the past-away, there may be then
No resurrection in the minds of men.

Who findeth comfort in the stars and flowers
Apparelling the earth and evening sky,
That moralize throughout their silent hours,
And woo us heaven-wards till we wish to die;
Oft hath he singled from the soothing quire,
For its calm influence, one of softest charm
To still his bosom's pangs, when they desire
A solace for the world's remorseless harm.
Yet they, since to be beautiful and bless
Is but their way of life, will still remain
Cupbearers to the bee in humbleness,
Or look untouched down through the moony rain,
Living and being worlds in bright content,
Ignorant, not in scorn, of his affection's bent.

ELIZABETH BARRETT BROWNING

I thought once how Theocritus had sung
Of the sweet years, the dear and wished-for years,
Who each one in a gracious hand appears
To bear a gift for mortals, old or young:
And, as I mused it in his antique tongue,
I saw, in gradual vision through my tears,
The sweet, sad years, the melancholy years,
Those of my own life, who by turns had flung
A shadow across me. Straightway I was 'ware,
So weeping, how a mystic Shape did move
Behind me, and drew me backward by the hair,
And a voice said in mastery while I strove,
'Guess now who holds thee?'—'Death,' I said. But, there,
The silver answer rang, . . . 'Not Death, but Love.'

Go from me. Yet I feel that I shall stand
Henceforward in thy shadow. Nevermore
Alone upon the threshold of my door
Of individual life, I shall command
The uses of my soul, nor lift my hand
Serenely in the sunshine as before,
Without the sense of that which I forbore, . . .
Thy touch upon the palm. The widest land
Doom takes to part us, leaves thy heart in mine
With pulses that beat double. What I do
And what I dream include thee, as the wine
Must taste of its own grapes. And when I sue
God for myself, He hears that name of thine,
And sees within my eyes the tears of two.

What can I give thee back, O liberal
And princely giver, who hast brought the gold
And purple of thine heart, unstained, untold,
And laid them on the outside of the wall
For such as I to take or leave withal,
In unexpected largesse? Am I cold,
Ungrateful, that for these most manifold
High gifts, I render nothing back at all?
Not so; not cold,—but very poor instead.
Ask God who knows. For frequent tears have run
The colours from my life, and left so dead
And pale a stuff, it were not fitly done
To give the same as pillow to thy head.
Go farther! let it serve to trample on.

If thou must love me, let it be for nought
Except for love's sake only. Do not say
'I love her for her smile . . . her look . . . her way
Of speaking gently, . . . for a trick of thought
That falls in well with mine, and certes brought
A sense of pleasant ease on such a day'—
For these things in themselves, Belovèd, may
Be changed, or change for thee,—and love, so wrought,
May be unwrought so. Neither love me for
Thine own dear pity's wiping my cheeks dry,—
A creature might forget to weep, who bore
Thy comfort long, and lose thy love thereby!
But love me for love's sake, that evermore
Thou may'st love on, through love's eternity.

When our two souls stand up erect and strong,
Face to face, silent, drawing nigh and nigher,
Until the lengthening wings break into fire
At either curvèd point,—what bitter wrong
Can the earth do to us, that we should not long
Be here contented? Think. In mounting higher,
The angels would press on us, and aspire
To drop some golden orb of perfect song
Into our deep, dear silence. Let us stay
Rather on earth, Belovèd,—where the unfit
Contrarious moods of men recoil away
And isolate pure spirits, and permit
A place to stand and love in for a day,
With darkness and the death-hour rounding it.

Autumn

Thou comest, Autumn, heralded by the rain,
  With banners, by great gales incessant fanned,
  Brighter than brightest silks of Samarcand,
  And stately oxen harnessed to thy wain;
Thou standest, like imperial Charlemagne,
  Upon thy bridge of gold; thy royal hand
  Outstretched with benedictions o'er the land,
  Blessing the farms through all thy vast domain.
Thy shield is the red harvest moon, suspended
  So long beneath the heaven's o'erhanging eaves;
Thy steps are by the farmer's prayers attended;
  Like flames upon an altar shine the sheaves;
And, following thee, in thy ovation splendid,
  Thine, almoner, the wind, scatters the golden leaves!

Chaucer

An old man in a lodge within a park;
  The chamber walls depicted all around
  With portraitures of huntsman, hawk, and hound,
  And the hurt deer. He listeneth to the lark,
Whose song comes with the sunshine through the dark
  Of painted glass in leaden lattice bound;
  He listeneth and he laugheth at the sound,
  Then writeth in a book like any clerk.
He is the poet of the dawn, who wrote
  The Canterbury Tales, and his old age
    Made beautiful with song; and as I read
I hear the crowing cock, I hear the note
  Of lark and linnet, and from every page
    Rise odours of ploughed field or flowery mead.

Divina Commedia

Oft have I seen at some cathedral door
   A labourer, pausing in the dust and heat,
   Lay down his burden, and with reverent feet
Enter, and cross himself, and on the floor
Kneel to repeat his Paternoster o'er:
   Far off the noises of the world retreat—
   The loud vociferations of the street
Become an indistinguishable roar.
So, as I enter here from day to day,
   And leave my burden at this minster gate,
Kneeling in prayer, and not ashamed to pray,
   The tumult of the time disconsolate
To inarticulate murmurs dies away,
   While the eternal ages watch and wait.

Nature

As a fond mother, when the day is o'er,
   Leads by the hand her little child to bed,
   Half willing, half reluctant to be led
And leave his broken playthings on the floor,
Still gazing at them through the open door,
   Not wholly reassured and comforted
   By promises of others in their stead,
Which, though more splendid, may not please him more;
So Nature deals with us, and takes away
   Our playthings one by one, and by the hand
   Leads us to rest so gently that we go
Scarce knowing if we wish to go or stay,
   Being too full of sleep to understand
   How the unknown transcends the what we know.

EDGAR ALLEN POE

An Enigma

'Seldom we find,' says Solomon Don Dunce,
　'Half an idea in the profoundest sonnet.
Through all the flimsy things we see at once
　As easily as through a Naples bonnet—
　Trash of all trash!—how *can* a lady don it?
Yet heavier far than your Petrarchan stuff—
Owl-downy nonsense that the faintest puff
　Twirls into trunk-paper the while you con it.'
And veritably, Sol is right enough.
　The general tuckermanities are arrant
　Bubbles—ephemeral and *so* transparent—
But *this* is, now—you may depend upon it—
　Stable, opaque, immortal—all by dint
　Of the dear names that lie concealed within't.

The concealed names become apparent if one takes the first letter of the first line, the second letter of the second, the third of third, and so on to the fourteenth.

GEORGE ELIOT

Brother and Sister

Long years have left their writing on my brow,
　But yet the freshness and the dew-fed beam
Of those young mornings are about me now,
　When we two wandered toward the far-off stream
With rod and line. Our basket held a store
　Baked for us only, and I thought with joy
That I should have my share, though he had more,
　Because he was the elder and a boy.
The firmaments of daisies since to me
　Have had those mornings in their opening eyes;
The bunchèd cowslip's pale transparency
　Carries that sunshine of sweet memories,
And wild-rose branches take their finest scent
From those blest hours of infantine content.

Shakespeare

Others abide our question—Thou art free!
    We ask and ask—Thou smilest and art still,
    Out-topping knowledge! So some sovran hill
Who to the stars uncrowns his majesty,
Planting his steadfast footsteps in the sea,
    Making the heaven of heavens his dwelling-place,
    Spares but the border, often, of his base
To the foiled searching of mortality;
And thou, whose head did stars and sunbeams know,
    Self-schooled, self-scanned, self-honoured, self-secure,
Didst walk on earth unguessed at.—Better so!
    All pains the immortal spirit must endure,
All weakness which impairs, all griefs which bow,
Find their sole voice in that victorious brow.

Quiet Work

One lesson, Nature, let me learn of thee,
    One lesson which in every wind is blown,
    One lesson of two duties kept at one
Though the loud world proclaim their enmity—
Of toil unsevered from tranquillity!
    Of labour, that in lasting fruit outgrows
    Far noisier schemes, accomplished in repose,
Too great for haste, too high for rivalry!

Yes, while on earth a thousand discords ring,
    Man's fitful uproar mingling with his toil,
      Still do thy sleepless ministers move on,
Their glorious tasks in silence perfecting;
    Still working, blaming still our vain turmoil,
      Labourers that shall not fail, when man is gone.

Written in Butler's Sermons

Affections, Instincts, Principles and Powers,
Impulse and Reason, Freedom and Control—
So men, unravelling God's harmonious whole,
Rend in a thousand shreds this life of ours.
Vain labour! Deep and broad, where none may see,
Spring the foundations of the shadowy throne
Where Man's one nature, queen-like, sits alone,
Centred in a majestic unity;
And rays her powers, like sister islands, seen
Linking their coral arms under the sea;
Or clustered peaks, with plunging gulfs between
Spanned by aerial arches, all of gold,
Whereo'er the chariot wheels of life are rolled
In cloudy circles, to eternity.

DANTE GABRIEL ROSSETTI

A sonnet is a moment's monument,—
   Memorial from the Soul's eternity
   To one dead deathless hour. Look that it be,
Whether for lustral rite or dire portent,
Of its own arduous fulness reverent:
   Carve it in ivory or in ebony,
   As Day or Night may rule; and let Time see
Its flowering crest impearled and orient.

A sonnet is a coin: its face reveals
   The soul,—its converse, to what Power 'tis due:—
Whether for tribute to the august appeals
   Of Life, or dower in Love's high retinue,
It serve; or, 'mid the dark wharf's cavernous breath,
In Charon's palm it pay the toll to Death.

Broken Music

The mother will not turn, who thinks she hears
    Her nursling's speech first grow articulate;
    But breathless with averted eyes elate
She sits, with open lips and open ears,
That it may call her twice. 'Mid doubts and fears
    Thus oft my soul has hearkened; till the song,
    A central moan for days, at length found tongue,
And the sweet music welled and the sweet tears.

But now, whatever while the soul is fain
    To list that wonted murmur, as it were
The speech-bound sea-shell's low importunate strain,—
    No breath of song, thy voice alone is there,
O bitterly beloved! and all her gain
    Is but the pang of unpermitted prayer.

Spring

Soft-littered is the new year's lambing-fold,
    And in the hollowed haystack at its side
    The shepherd lies o'nights now, wakeful-eyed
At the ewes' travailing call through the dark cold.
The young rooks cheep 'mid the thick caw o' the old:
    And near unpeopled stream-sides, on the ground,
    By her spring-cry the moorhen's nest is found,
Where the drained flood-lands flaunt their marigold.
Chill are the gusts to which the pastures cower,
    And chill the current where the young reeds stand
    As green and close as the young wheat on land:
Yet here the cuckoo and the cuckoo-flower
Plight to the heart Spring's perfect imminent hour
    Whose breath shall soothe you like your dear one's hand

Hope Overtaken

I deemed thy garments, O my Hope, were grey,
    So far I viewed thee. Now the space between
    Is passed at length; and garmented in green
Even as in days of yore thou stand'st today.
Ah God! and but for lingering dull dismay,
    On all that road our footsteps erst had been
    Even thus commingled, and our shadows seen
Blent on the hedgerows and the water-way.

O Hope of mine, whose eyes are living love,
    No eyes but hers,—O Love and Hope the same!—
    Lean close to me, for now the sinking sun
That warmed our feet scarce gilds our hair above.
    O hers thy voice and very hers thy name!
    Alas, cling round me, for the day is done!

On Refusal of Aid Between Nations

Not that the earth is changing, O my God!
    Nor that the seasons totter in their walk,—
    Not that the virulent ill of act and talk
Seethes ever as a winepress ever trod,—
Not therefore are we certain that the rod
    Weighs in thine hand to smite thy world; though now
    Beneath thine hand so many nations bow,
So many kings:—not therefore, O my God!—

But because Man is parcelled out in men
    Even thus; because, for any wrongful blow,
    No man not stricken asks, 'I would be told
Why thou dost strike;' but his heart whispers then,
    'He is he, I am I.' By this we know
    That the earth falls asunder, being old.

Barren Spring

Once more the changed year's turning wheel returns:
　　And as a girl sails balanced in the wind,
　　And now before and now again behind
Stoops as it swoops, with cheek that laughs and burns,—
　　So Spring comes merry towards me now, but earns
　　　　No answering smile from me, whose life is twined
　　　　With the dead boughs that winter still must bind,
　　And whom to-day the Spring no more concerns.

Behold, this crocus is a withering flame;
　　This snowdrop, snow; this apple-blossom's part
　　To breed the fruit that breeds the serpent's art.
Nay, for these Spring-flowers, turn thy face from them,
Nor gaze till on the year's last lily-stem
　　The white cup shrivels round the golden heart.

GEORGE MEREDITH

We saw the swallows gathering in the sky,
And in the osier-isle we heard them noise.
We had not to look back on summer joys,
Or forward to a summer of bright dye:
But in the largeness of the evening earth
Our spirits grew as we went side by side.
The hour became her husband and my bride.
Love that had robbed us so, thus blessed our dearth!
The pilgrims of the year waxed very loud
In multitudinous chatterings, as the flood
Full brown came from the West, and like pale blood
Expanded to the upper crimson cloud.
Love that had robbed us of immortal things,
This little moment mercifully gave,
Where I have seen across the twilight wave
The swan sail with her young beneath her wings.

Lucifer in Starlight

On a starred night Prince Lucifer uprose.
Tired of his dark dominion swung the fiend
Above the rolling ball in cloud part screened,
Where sinners hugged their spectre of repose.
Poor prey to his hot fit of pride were those.
And now upon his western wing he leaned,
Now his huge bulk o'er Afric's sands careened,
Now the black planet shadowed Arctic snows.
Soaring through wider zones that pricked his scars
With memory of the old revolt from Awe,
He reached a middle height, and at the stars,
Which are the brain of heaven, he looked, and sank.
Around the ancient track marched rank on rank
The army of unalterable law.

Earth's Secret

Not solitarily in fields we find
Earth's secret open, though one page is there;
Her plainest, such as children spell, and share
With bird and beast; raised letters for the blind.
Not where the troubled passions toss the mind,
In turbid cities, can the key be bare.
It hangs for those who hither thither fare,
Close interthreading nature with our kind.
They, hearing History speak, of what men were,
And have become, are wise. The gain is great
In vision and solidity; it lives.
Yet at a thought of life apart from her,
Solidity and vision lose their state,
For Earth, that gives the milk, the spirit gives.

After Death

The curtains were half drawn, the floor was swept
  And strewn with rushes, rosemary and may
  Lay thick upon the bed on which I lay,
Where through the lattice ivy-shadows crept.
He leaned above me, thinking that I slept
  And could not hear him; but I heard him say,
  'Poor child, poor child': and as he turned away
Came a deep silence, and I knew he wept.
He did not touch the shroud, or raise the fold
  That hid my face, or take my hand in his,
    Or ruffle the smooth pillows for my head:
    He did not love me living; but once dead
  He pitied me; and very sweet it is
To know he still is warm though I am dead.

Remember

Remember me when I am gone away,
  Gone far away into the silent land;
  When you can no more hold me by the hand,
Nor I half turn to go yet turning stay.
Remember me when no more day by day
  You tell me of our future that you planned:
  Only remember me; you understand
It will be late to counsel then or pray.
Yet if you should forget me for a while
  And afterwards remember, do not grieve:
  For if the darkness and corruption leave
  A vestige of the thoughts that once I had,
Better by far you should forget and smile
  Than that you should remember and be sad.

RICHARD WATSON DIXON

There is a soul above the soul of each,
A mightier soul, which yet to each belongs:
There is a sound made of all human speech,
And numerous as the concourse of all songs:
And in that soul lives each, in each that soul,
Though all the ages are its lifetime vast;
Each soul that dies, in its most sacred whole
Receiveth life that shall for ever last.

   And thus for ever with a wider span
Humanity o'erarches time and death;
Man can elect the universal man,
And live in life that ends not with his breath,
And gather glory that increaseth still
Till Time his glass with Death's last dust shall fill.

JAMES THOMSON (B.V.)

Striving to sing glad songs, I but attain
Wild discords sadder than grief's saddest tune,
As if an owl, with his harsh screech, should strain
To overgratulate a thrush of June.
The nightingale upon its thorny spray
Finds inspiration in the sullen dark:
The kindling dawn, the world-wide joyous day,
Are inspiration to the soaring lark.
The seas are silent in the sunny calm;
Their anthem-surges in the tempest boom.
The skies outroll no solemn thunder psalm
Till they have clothed themselves with clouds of gloom.
My mirth can laugh and talk, but cannot sing;
My grief finds harmonies in everything.

My Heart is Vexed

My heart is vexed with this fantastic fear,—
Had I been born too soon, or far away,
Then had I never known thy beauty, dear,
And thou hadst spent on others all thy May.
The idle thought can freeze an idle brain
Faint at imagined loss of such dear prize;
I pore upon the slender chance again,
That taught me all the meaning of those eyes.
But creeps a whisper with a treason tongue—
Hadst never sunned beneath this maiden's glance
Another love thou hadst as madly sung,
For love is certain but the loved one chance.
  Deject and doubtful thus I forge quaint fear,
  But question little, love, when thou art near.

SAMUEL BUTLER

The Life After Death

Not on sad Stygian shore, nor in clear sheen
Of far Elysian plain, shall we meet those
Among the dead whose pupils we have been,
Nor those great shades whom we have held as foes;
No meadow of asphodel our feet shall tread,
Nor shall we look each other in the face
To love or hate each other being dead,
Hoping some praise or fearing some disgrace.
We shall not argue saying ''Twas thus' or 'Thus',
Our argument's whole drift we shall forget;
Who's right, who's wrong, 'twill be all one to us;
We shall not even know that we have met.
  Yet meet we shall, and part, and meet again,
  Where dead men meet, on lips of living men.

Esther

When I hear laughter from a tavern door,
 When I see crowds agape and in the rain
Watching on tiptoe and with stifled roar
 To see a rocket fired or a bull slain,
When misers handle gold, when orators
 Touch strong men's hearts with glory till they weep,
When cities deck their streets for barren wars
 Which have laid waste their youth, and when I keep
Calmly the count of my own life and see
 On what poor stuff my manhood's dreams were fed
Till I too learned what dole of vanity
 Will serve a human soul for daily bread,
—Then I remember that I once was young
And lived with Esther the world's gods among.

Honour Dishonoured

('Written in an Irish Prison 1888')

Honoured I lived e'erwhile with honoured men
 In opulent state. My table nightly spread
Found guests of worth, peer, priest and citizen,
 And poet crowned, and beauty garlanded.
 Nor these alone, for hunger too I fed,
And many a lean tramp and sad Magdalen
 Passed from my doors less hard for sake of bread.
Whom grudged I ever purse or hand or pen?

Tonight, unwelcomed at these gates of woe
 I stand with churls, and there is none to greet
My weariness with smile or courtly show
 Nor, though I hunger long, to bring me meat.
God! what a little accident of gold
Fences our weakness from the wolves of old!

Depreciating her Beauty

I love not thy perfections. When I hear
Thy beauty blazoned, and the common tongue
Cheapening with vulgar praise a lip, an ear,
A cheek that I have prayed to;—when among
The loud world's gods my god is noised and sung,
Her wit applauded, even her taste, her dress,
Her each dear hidden marvel lightly flung
At the world's feet and stripped to nakedness—
Then I despise thy beauty utterly,
Crying, 'Be these your gods, O Israel!'
And I remember that on such a day
I found thee with eyes bleared and cheeks all pale,
And lips that trembled to a voiceless cry,
And that thy bosom in my bosom lay.

THOMAS HARDY

Hap

If but some vengeful god would call to me
From up the sky, and laugh: 'Thou suffering thing,
Know that thy sorrow is my ecstasy,
That thy love's loss is my hate's profiting!'

Then would I bear, and clench myself, and die,
Steeled by the sense of ire unmerited;
Half-eased in that a Powerfuller than I
Had willed and meted me the tears I shed.

But not so. How arrives it joy lies slain,
And why unblooms the best hope ever sown?
—Crass Casualty obstructs the sun and rain,
And dicing Time for gladness casts a moan. . .
These purblind Doomsters had as readily strown
Blisses about my pilgrimage as pain.

She, to Him

Perhaps, long hence, when I have passed away,
Some other's feature, accent, thought like mine,
Will carry you back to what I used to say,
And bring some memory of your love's decline.

Then you may pause awhile and think, 'Poor jade!'
And yield a sigh to me—as ample due,
Not as the title of a debt unpaid
To one who could resign her all to you—

And thus reflecting, you will never see
That your thin thought, in two small words conveyed,
Was no such fleeting phantom-thought to me,
But the Whole Life wherein my part was played;
And you amid its fitful masquerade
A Thought—as I in yours but seem to be.

To a Lady
Offended by a Book of the Writer's

Now that my page upcloses, doomed, maybe,
Never to press thy cosy cushions more,
Or wake thy ready Yeas as heretofore,
Or stir thy gentle vows of faith in me:

Knowing thy natural receptivity,
I figure that, as flambeaux banish eve,
My sombre image, warped by insidious heave
Of those less forthright, must lose place in thee.

So be it. I have borne such. Let thy dreams
Of me and mine diminish day by day,
And yield their space to shine of smugger things;
Till I shape to thee but in fitful gleams,
And then in far and feeble visitings,
And then surcease. Truth will be truth alway.

FREDERIC WILLIAM HENRY MYERS

Would God It Were Morning

My God, how many times ere I be dead
    Must I the bitterness of dying know?
How often like a corpse upon my bed
    Compose me and surrender me and so
Through hateful hours and ill-rememberèd
    Between the twilight and the twilight go,
By visions bodiless obscurely led
    Through many a wild enormity of woe?
And yet I know not but that this is worst,
When with that light, the feeble and the first,
    I start and gaze into the world again,
And gazing find it as of old accurst
And grey and blinded with the stormy burst
    And blank appalling solitude of rain.

GERARD MANLEY HOPKINS

God's Grandeur

The world is charged with the grandeur of God.
    It will flame out, like shining from shook foil;
    It gathers to a greatness, like the ooze of oil
Crushed. Why do men then now not reck his rod?
Generations have trod, have trod, have trod;
    And all is seared with trade; bleared, smeared with toil;
    And wears man's smudge and shares man's smell: the soil
Is bare now, nor can foot feel, being shod.

And for all this, nature is never spent;
    There lives the dearest freshness deep down things;
And though the last lights off the black West went
    Oh, morning, at the brown brink eastward, springs—
Because the Holy Ghost over the bent
    World broods with warm breast and with ah! bright
        wings.

Pied Beauty

Glory be to God for dappled things—
    For skies of couple-colour as a brinded cow;
      For rose-moles all in stipple upon trout that swim;
Fresh-firecoal chestnut-falls; finches' wings;
    Landscape plotted and pieced—fold, fallow, and plough;
      And all trades, their gear and tackle and trim.
All things counter, original, spare, strange;
    Whatever is fickle, freckled (who knows how?)
      With swift, slow; sweet, sour; adazzle, dim;
He fathers-forth whose beauty is past change:
          Praise him.

Hurrahing in Harvest

Summer ends now; now, barbarous in beauty, the stooks
    arise
    Around; up above, what wind-walks! what lovely
    behaviour
    Of silk-sack clouds! has wilder, wilful-wavier
Meal-drift moulded ever and melted across skies?

I walk, I lift up, I lift up heart, eyes,
    Down all that glory in the heavens to glean our Saviour;
    And, eyes, heart, what looks, what lips yet gave you a
Rapturous love's greeting of realer, of rounder replies?

And the azurous hung hills are his world-wielding shoulder
    Majestic—as a stallion stalwart, very-violet-sweet!—
These things, these things were here and but the beholder
    Wanting; which two when they once meet,
The heart rears wings bold and bolder
    And hurls for him, O half hurls earth for him off under
    his feet

Felix Randal

FELIX RANDAL the farrier, O he is dead then? my duty all
　　ended,
Who have watched his mould of man, big-boned and
　　hardy-handsome
Pining, pining, till time when reason rambled in it and some
Fatal four disorders, fleshed there, all contended?

Sickness broke him. Impatient he cursed at first, but
　　mended
Being anointed and all; though a heavenlier heart began
　　some
Months earlier, since I had our sweet reprieve and ransom
Tendered to him. Ah well, God rest him and all road ever
　　he offended!

This seeing the sick endears them to us, us too it endears.
My tongue had taught thee comfort, touch had quenched
　　thy tears,
Thy tears that touched my heart, child, Felix, poor Felix
　　Randal;

How far from then forethought of, all thy more boisterous
　　years,
When thou at the random grim forge, powerful amidst
　　peers,
Didst fettle for the great grey drayhorse his bright and
　　battering sandal!

No worst, there is none. Pitched past pitch of grief,
More pangs will, schooled at forepangs, wilder wring.
Comforter, where, where is your comforting?
Mary, mother of us, where is your relief?
My cries heave, herds-long; huddle in a main, a chief
Woe, world-sorrow; on an age-old anvil wince and sing—
Then lull, then leave off. Fury had shrieked 'No ling-
ering! Let me be fell: force I must be brief'.

O the mind, mind has mountains; cliffs of fall
Frightful, sheer, no-man-fathomed. Hold them cheap
May who ne'er hung there. Nor does long our small
Durance deal with that steep or deep. Here! creep,
Wretch, under a comfort serves in a whirlwind: all
Life death does end and each day dies with sleep.

Spring

Nothing is so beautiful as spring—
    When weeds, in wheels, shoot long and lovely and
      lush;
    Thrush's eggs look little low heavens, and thrush
Through the echoing timber does so rinse and wring
The ear, it strikes like lightnings to hear him sing;
    The glassy peartree leaves and blooms, they brush
    The descending blue; that blue is all in a rush
With richness; the racing lambs too have fair their fling.

What is all this juice and all this joy?
    A strain of the earth's sweet being in the beginning
In Eden garden.—Have, get, before it cloy,
    Before it cloud, Christ, lord, and sour with sinning,
Innocent mind and Mayday in girl and boy,
    Most, O maid's child, thy choice and worthy the
      winning.

The Windhover

To Christ our Lord

I caught this morning morning's minion, king-
  dom of daylight's dauphin, dapple-dawn-drawn
    Falcon, in his riding
Of the rolling level underneath him steady air, and striding
High there, how he rung upon the rein of a wimpling wing
In his ecstasy! then off, off forth on swing,
  As a skate's heel sweeps smooth on a bow-bend: the hurl
    and gliding
Rebuffed the big wind. My heart in hiding
Stirred for a bird,—the achieve of, the mastery of the thing!

Brute beauty and valour and act, oh, air, pride, plume, here
  Buckle! AND the fire that breaks from thee then, a billion
Times told lovelier, more dangerous, O my chevalier!

  No wonder of it: sheer plod makes plough down sillion
Shine, and blue-bleak embers, ah my dear,
  Fall, gall themselves, and gash gold-vermilion.

  Thou art indeed just, Lord, if I contend
  With thee; but, sir, so what I plead is just.
  Why do sinners' ways prosper? and why must
  Disappointment all I endeavour end?
    Wert thou my enemy, O thou my friend,
  How wouldst thou worse, I wonder, than thou dost
  Defeat, thwart me? Oh, the sots and thralls of lust
  Do in spare hours more thrive than I that spend,
  Sir, life upon thy cause. See, banks and brakes
  Now, leavèd how thick! lacèd they are again
  With fretty chervil, look, and fresh wind shakes
  Them; birds build—but not I build; no, but strain,
  Time's eunuch, and not breed one work that wakes.
  Mine, O thou lord of life, send my roots rain.

The Sea and the Skylark

On ear and ear two noises too old to end
　　Trench—right, the tide that ramps against the shore;
　　With a flood or a fall, low lull-off or all roar,
Frequenting there while moon shall wear and wend.

Left hand, off land, I hear the lark ascend,
　　His rash-fresh re-winded new-skeinèd score
　　In crisps of curl off wild winch whirl, and pour
And pelt music, till none's to spill nor spend.

How these two shame this shallow and frail town!
　　How ring right out our sordid turbid time,
Being pure! We, life's pride and cared-for crown,

　　Have lost that cheer and charm of earth's past prime:
Our make and making break, are breaking, down
　　To man's last dust, drain fast towards man's first slime.

The Odyssey

As one that for a weary space has lain
　　Lulled by the song of Circe and her wine
　　In gardens near the pale of Proserpine,
Where that Æean isle forgets the main,
And only the low lutes of love complain,
　　And only shadows of wan lovers pine—
　　As such an one were glad to know the brine
Salt on his lips, and the large air again,—
So gladly, from the songs of modern speech
　　Men turn, and see the stars, and feel the free
　　　Shrill wind beyond the close of heavy flowers,
　　　And through the music of the languid hours
They hear like Ocean on the western beach
　　The surge and thunder of the Odyssey.

ANDREW LANG

Herodotus in Egypt

He left the land of youth, he left the young,
  The smiling gods of Greece; he passed the isle
Where Jason loitered, and where Sappho sung;
  He sought the secret-founted wave of Nile,
  And of their old world, dead a weary while,
Heard the priests murmur in their mystic tongue,
And through the fanes went voyaging, among
  Dark tribes that worshipped Cat and Crocodile.
He learned the tales of death Divine and birth,
Strange loves of Hawk and Serpent, Sky and Earth,
  The marriage, and the slaying of the Sun.
The shrines of gods and beasts he wandered through,
And mocked not at their godhead, for he knew
  Behind all creeds the Spirit that is One.

ROBERT BRIDGES

The work is done, and from the fingers fall
The bloodwarm tools that brought the labour thro':
The tasking eye that overrunneth all
Rests, and affirms there is no more to do.
  Now the third joy of making, the sweet flower
Of blessed work, bloometh in godlike spirit;
Which whoso plucketh holdeth for an hour
The shrivelling vanity of mortal merit.

  And thou, my perfect work, thou'rt of to-day;
To-morrow a poor and alien thing wilt be,
True only should the swift life stand at stay:
Therefore farewell, nor look to bide with me.
  Go find thy friends, if there be one to love thee:
Casting thee forth, my child, I rise above thee.

The fabled sea-snake, old Leviathan,
Or else what grisly beast of scaly chine
That champed the ocean-wrack and swashed the brine,
Before the new and milder days of man,
Had never rib nor bray nor swindging fan
Like his iron swimmer of the Clyde or Tyne,
Late-born of golden seed to breed a line
Of offspring swifter and more huge of plan.

Straight is her going, for upon the sun
When once she hath looked, her path and place are plain;
With tireless speed she smiteth one by one
The shuddering seas and foams along the main;
And her eased breath, when her wild race is run,
Roars thro' her nostrils like a hurricane.

My lady pleases me and I please her;
This know we both, and I besides know well
Wherefore I love her, and I love to tell
My love, as all my loving songs aver.
But what on her part could the passion stir,
Tho' 'tis more difficult for love to spell,
Yet can I dare divine how this befel,
Nor will her lips deny it if I err.

She loves me first because I love her, then
Loves me for knowing why she should be loved,
And that I love to praise her, loves again.
So from her beauty both our loves are moved,
And by her beauty are sustained; nor when
The earth falls from the sun is this disproved.

I care not if I live, tho' life and breath
　　Have never been to me so dear and sweet.
　　I care not if I die, for I could meet—
Being so happy—happily my death.
I care not if I love; to-day she saith
　　She loveth, and love's history is complete.
　　Nor care I if she love me; at her feet
My spirit bows entranced and worshippeth.
I have no care for what was most my care,
　　But all around me see fresh beauty born,
And common sights grown lovelier than they were:
　　I dream of love, and in the light of morn
Tremble, beholding all things very fair
　　And strong with strength that puts my strength to scorn.

OSCAR WILDE

Written in Holy Week at Genoa

I wandered through Scoglietto's far retreat,
　　The oranges on each o'erhanging spray
　　Burned as bright lamps of gold to shame the day;
Some startled bird with fluttering wings and fleet
Made snow of all the blossoms; at my feet
　　Like silver moons the pale narcissi lay:
　　And the curved waves that streaked the great green bay
Laughed in the sun; and life seemed very sweet.
Outside the young boy-priest passed singing clear,
　　'Jesus the son of Mary has been slain,
　　O come and fill his sepulchre with flowers.'
Ah, God! Ah, God! those dear Hellenic hours
　　Had drowned all memory of Thy bitter pain,
　　The Cross, the Crown, the Soldiers and the Spear.

166

Santa Decca

The Gods are dead: no longer do we bring
　　To grey-eyed Pallas crowns of olive-leaves!
　　Demeter's child no more hath tithe of sheaves,
And in the noon the careless shepherds sing,
For Pan is dead, and all the wantoning
　　By secret glade and devious haunt is o'er:
　　Young Hylas seeks the water-springs no more;
Great Pan is dead, and Mary's son is King.

And yet—perchance in this sea-trancèd isle,
　　Chewing the bitter fruit of memory,
　　Some God lies hidden in the asphodel.
Ah Love! if such there be, then it were well
　　For us to fly his anger: nay, but see,
　　The leaves are stirring: let us watch awhile.

Corfu.

To Liberty

Not that I love thy children, whose dull eyes
See nothing save their own unlovely woe,
Whose minds know nothing, nothing care to know,—
But that the roar of thy Democracies,
Thy reigns of Terror, thy great Anarchies,
Mirror my wildest passions like the sea
And give my rage a brother—Liberty!
For this sake only do thy dissonant cries
Delight my discreet soul, else might all kings
By bloody knout or treacherous cannonades
Rob nations of their rights inviolate
And I remain unmoved—and yet, and yet,
These Christs that die upon the barricades,
God knows it I am with them, in some things.

Impression de Voyage

The sea was sapphire coloured, and the sky
   Burned like a heated opal through the air;
   We hoisted sail; the wind was blowing fair
For the blue lands that to the eastward lie.
From the steep prow I marked with quickening eye
   Zakynthos, every olive grove and creek,
   Ithaca's cliff, Lycaon's snowy peak,
And all the flower-strewn hills of Arcady.
The flapping of the sail against the mast,
   The ripple of the water on the side,
   The ripple of girls' laughter at the stern,
The only sounds:—when 'gan the West to burn,
   And a red sun upon the seas to ride,
   I stood upon the soil of Greece at last!

SIR WILLIAM WATSON

In City Pent

O sweet at this sweet hour to wander free,
   Or follow some invisible-beckoning hand,
   Among the moody mountains, where they stand
Awed with the thought of their own majesty!
Sweet, at the folding up of day, to be
   Where, on the tattered fringes of the land,
   The uncourted flowers of the penurious sand
Are pale against the pale lips of the sea.
Sweetest to dream, on easeful earth reclined,
   Far in some forest's ancient idleness,
     Under the shadow of its bossy boles;
   Beyond the world's pursuit, and Care's access;
And hear the wild feet of the elfin wind
     Dancing and prancing in mad caprioles.

FRANCIS THOMPSON

Ad Amicam

Dear Dove, that bear'st to my sole-labouring ark
    The olive-branch of so long wishèd rest,
When the white solace glimmers through my dark
    Of nearing wings, what comfort in my breast!
Oh, may that doubted day not come, not come,
    When you shall fail, my heavenly messenger,
And drift into the distance and the doom
    Of all my impermissible things that were!
Rather than so, now make the sad farewell,
    Which yet may be with not too-painèd pain,
Lest I again the acquainted tale should tell
    Of sharpest loss that pays for shortest gain.
      Ah, if my heart should hear no white wings thrill
      Against its waiting window, open still!

WILLIAM BUTLER YEATS

The Folly of being Comforted

One that is ever kind said yesterday:
'Your well-belovèd's hair has threads of grey,
And little shadows come about her eyes;
Time can but make it easier to be wise
Though now it seems impossible, and so
All that you need is patience.'
                Heart cries, 'No,
I have not a crumb of comfort, not a grain.
Time can but make her beauty over again:
Because of that great nobleness of hers
The fire that stirs about her, when she stirs,
Burns but more clearly. O she had not these ways
When all the wild summer was in her gaze.'

O heart! O heart! if she'd but turn her head,
You'd know the folly of being comforted.

The Fascination of What's Difficult

The fascination of what's difficult
Has dried the sap out of my veins, and rent
Spontaneous joy and natural content
Out of my heart. There's something ails our colt
That must, as if it had not holy blood
Nor on Olympus leaped from cloud to cloud,
Shiver under the lash, strain, sweat and jolt
As though it dragged road metal. My curse on plays
That have to be set up in fifty ways,
On the day's war with every knave and dolt,
Theatre business, management of men.
I swear before the dawn comes round again
I'll find the stable and pull out the bolt.

LIONEL JOHNSON

The night is full of stars, full of magnificence;
    Nightingales hold the wood, and fragrance loads the dark.
    Behold what fires august, what lights eternal! Hark!
What passionate music poured in passionate love's defence.
Breathe but the wafting wind's nocturnal frankincense!
    Only to feel this night's great heart, only to mark
    The splendours and the glooms, brings back the
        patriarch
Who on Chaldæan wastes found God through reverence.

Could we but live at will upon this perfect height,
    Could we but always keep the passion of this peace,
Could we but face unshamed the look of this pure light,
    Could we but win earth's heart and give desire release,
Then were we all divine, and then were ours by right
These stars, these nightingales, these scents; then shame
        would cease.

Forgetfulness

Alas! that Time should war against Distress,
And numb the sweet ache of remembered loss,
And give for sorrow's gold the indifferent dross
Of calm regret or stark forgetfulness.
I should have worn eternal mourning dress
And nailed my soul to some perennial cross,
And made my thoughts like restless waves that toss
On the wild sea's intemperate wilderness.

But lo! came Life, and with its painted toys
Lured me to play again like any child.
O pardon me this weak inconstancy.
May my soul die if in all present joys,
Lapped in forgetfulness or sense-beguiled
Yea, in my mirth, if I prefer not thee.

JOHN MASEFIELD

Here in the self is all that man can know
Of Beauty, all the wonder, all the power,
All the unearthly colour, all the glow,
Here in the self which withers like a flower;
Here in the self which fades as hours pass,
And droops and dies and rots and is forgotten
Sooner, by ages, than the mirroring glass
In which it sees its glory still unrotten.
Here in the flesh, within the flesh, behind,
Swift in the blood and throbbing on the bone,
Beauty herself, the universal mind,
Eternal April wandering alone;
The God, the holy Ghost, the atoning Lord,
Here in the flesh, the never yet explored.

Let that which is to come be as it may,
Darkness, extinction, justice, life intense,
The flies are happy in the summer day,
Flies will be happy many summers hence.
Time with his antique breeds that built the Sphinx,
Time with her men to come whose wings will tower,
Poured and will pour, not as the wise man thinks,
But with blind force, to each his little hour.
And when the hour has struck, comes death or change,
Which, whether good or ill we cannot tell,
But the blind planet will wander through her range
Bearing men like us who will serve as well.
The sun will rise, the winds that ever move
Will blow our dust that once were men in love.

LASCELLES ABERCROMBIE

The Fear

As over muddy shores a dragon flock
   Went, in an early age from ours discrete,
    Before the grim race found oblivion meet;
And as Time hardened into iron rock
That unclean mud, and into cliffs did lock
   The story of those terrifying feet
    With hookèd claws and wrinkled scale complete,
Till quarrying startles us with amaz'd shock:

So there was something wont to pass along
   The plashy marge of early consciousness.
Now the quagmires are turned to pavement strong;
Those outer twilight regions bold I may
   Explore,—yet still I shudder with distress
To find detested tracks of his old way.

Epitaph

Sir, you should notice me: I am the Man;
I am Good Fortune: I am satisfied.
All I desired, more than I could desire,
I have: everything has gone right with me.
Life was a hiding-place that played me false;
I croucht ashamed, and still was seen and scorned:
But now I am not seen. I was a fool,
And now I know what wisdom dare not know:
For I know Nothing. I was a slave, and now
I have ungoverned freedom and the wealth
That cannot be conceived: for I have Nothing.
I lookt for beauty and I longed for rest,
And now I have perfection: nay, I am
Perfection: I am Nothing, I am dead.

JOHN DRINKWATER

We have laid up simples against forgetfulness,
For we the nesting missel thrush have seen
Brooding above the weaving watercress;
We have gone by water-meadows fresh and green
Studded with kingcups and with cuckoo-flowers,
By hedges newly fledged with blackthorn foam,
And rested, weary with the happy hours,
At twilight by the kindled hearth of home.

This was our spring, our lucky Eastertide,
By willowed brooks, and from a western shire
We shared a Monday of the undaunted pride
Of him who sang the old, the heart's desire;
England we were; and yet of England own
The budding bough, the song, the builded stone.

Prolegomena to any Future Satire

'Milton! thou shouldst be living at this hour,'
   but since your voice is still, and no one knows
whether life wears an artificial flower,
   or the deep velvet of a breathing rose,
since no one cares whether the sudden shower,
   that sweeps the world, is from a garden-hose,
or is the ancient, unexhausted power
   of rain that cleans, and sanctifies, and goes,

let me, as when by innocent sacrilege
   in some carved temple, whose hushed worshippers
seek truth, through Buddha's lips a wandered midge
   shrills and is quiet, so let me rehearse
as shrill and brief, but no less dedicate;
   'They also serve, who only stand and hate.'

This is the horror that, night after night,
   Sits grinning on my pillow—that I meant
   To mix the peace of being innocent
With the warm thrill of seeking out delight:
This is the final blasphemy, the blight
   On all pure purpose and divine intent—
   To dress the selfish thought, the indolent,
In the priest's sable or the angel's white.

For God's sake, if you sin, take pleasure in it,
   And do it for the pleasure. Do not say:
'Behold the spirit's liberty!—a minute
   Will see the earthly vesture break away
And God shine through.' Say: 'Here's a sin—I'll sin it;
And there's the price of sinning—and I'll pay.'

Dreamers

Soldiers are citizens of death's grey land,
 Drawing no dividend from time's to-morrows.
In the great hour of destiny they stand,
 Each with his feuds, and jealousies, and sorrows.
Soldiers are sworn to action; they must win
 Some flaming, fatal climax with their lives.
Soldiers are dreamers; when the guns begin
 They think of firelit homes, clean beds, and wives.

I see them in foul dug-outs, gnawed by rats,
 And in the ruined trenches, lashed with rain,
Dreaming of things they did with balls and bats,
 And mocked by hopeless longing to regain
Bank-holidays, and picture shows, and spats,
 And going to the office in the train.

The Glory of Women

You love us when we're heroes, home on leave,
Or wounded in a mentionable place.
You worship decorations; you believe
That chivalry redeems the war's disgrace.
You make us shells. You listen with delight,
By tales of dirt and danger fondly thrilled.
You crown our distant ardours while we fight,
And mourn our laurelled memories when we're killed.

You can't believe that British troops 'retire'
When hell's last horror breaks them, and they run,
Trampling the terrible corpses—blind with blood.
O German mother dreaming by the fire,
While you are knitting socks to send your son,
His face is trodden deeper in the mud.

Strangeness of Heart

When I have lost the power to feel the pang
Which first I felt in childhood when I woke
And heard the unheeding garden bird who sang
Strangeness of heart for me while morning broke;
Or when in latening twilight sure with spring,
Pausing on homeward paths along the wood,
No sadness thrills my thought while thrushes sing,
And I'm no more the listening child who stood
So many sunsets past and could not say
What wandering voices called from far away:
 When I have lost those simple spells that stirred
 My being with an untranslated song,
 Let me go home for ever; I shall have heard
 Death; I shall know that I have lived too long.

On Passing the New Menin Gate

Who will remember, passing through this Gate,
The unheroic Dead who fed the guns?
Who shall absolve the foulness of their fate,—
Those doomed, conscripted, unvictorious ones?
 Crudely renewed, the Salient holds its own.
 Paid are its dim defenders by this pomp;
 Paid, with a pile of peace-complacent stone,
 The armies who endured that sullen swamp.

Here was the world's worst wound. And here with pride
'Their name liveth for ever,' the Gateway claims.
Was ever an immolation so belied
As these intolerably nameless names?
Well might the Dead who struggled in the slime
Rise and deride this sepulchre of crime.

Oh, Death will find me, long before I tire
    Of watching you; and swing me suddenly
Into the shade and loneliness and mire
    Of the last land! There, waiting patiently,

One day, I think, I'll feel a cool wind blowing,
    See a slow light across the Stygian tide,
And hear the Dead about me stir, unknowing,
    And tremble. And I shall know that you have died,

And watch you, a broad-browed and smiling dream,
    Pass, light as ever, through the lightless host,
Quietly ponder, start, and sway, and gleam—
    Most individual and bewildering ghost!—

And turn, and toss your brown delightful head
Amusedly, among the ancient Dead.

The Dead II

These hearts were woven of human joys and cares,
Washed marvellously with sorrow, swift to mirth.
The years had given them kindness. Dawn was theirs,
And sunset and the colours of the earth.
These had seen movement, and heard music; known
Slumber and waking; loved; gone proudly friended;
Felt the quick stir of wonder; sat alone;
Touched flowers and furs, and cheeks. All this is ended.

There are waters blown by changing winds to laughter
And lit by the rich skies, all day. And after,
Frost, with a gesture, stays the waves that dance
And wandering loveliness. He leaves a white
Unbroken glory, a gathered radiance,
A width, a shining peace, under the night.

Failure

Because God put His adamantine fate
  Between my sullen heart and its desire,
I swore that I would burst the Iron Gate,
  Rise up, and curse Him on His throne of fire.
Earth shuddered at my crown of blasphemy,
  But Love was as a flame about my feet;
  Proud up the Golden Stair I strode; and beat
Thrice on the Gate, and entered with a cry—

All the great courts were quiet in the sun,
  And full of vacant echoes: moss had grown
Over the glassy pavement, and begun
  To creep within the dusty council-halls.
An idle wind blew round an empty throne
  And stirred the heavy curtains on the walls.

The Hill

Breathless, we flung us on the windy hill
  Laughed in the sun, and kissed the lovely grass.
  You said, 'Through glory and ecstasy we pass;
Wind, sun, and earth remain, the birds sing still,
When we are old, are old . . .' 'And when we die
  All's over that is ours; and life burns on
Through other lovers, other lips,' said I,
  'Heart of my heart, our heaven is now, is won!'

'We are Earth's best, that learnt her lesson here.
  Life is our cry. We have kept the faith!' we said;
  'We shall go down with unreluctant tread
Rose-crowned into the darkness!' . . . Proud we were,
And laughed, that had such brave true things to say.
—And then you suddenly cried, and turned away.

The Soldier

If I should die, think only this of me:
  That there's some corner of a foreign field
That is for ever England. There shall be
  In that rich earth a richer dust concealed;
A dust whom England bore, shaped, made aware,
  Gave, once, her flowers to love, her ways to roam,
A body of England's, breathing English air,
  Washed by the rivers, blest by suns of home.

And think, this heart, all evil shed away,
  A pulse in the eternal mind, no less
    Gives somewhere back the thoughts by England
      given;
Her sights and sounds; dreams happy as her day;
  And laughter, learnt of friends; and gentleness,
    In hearts at peace, under an English heaven.

Clouds

Down the blue night the unending columns press
  In noiseless tumult, break and wave and flow,
  Now tread the far South, or lift rounds of snow
Up to the white moon's hidden loveliness.
Some pause in their grave wandering comradeless,
  And turn with profound gesture vague and slow,
  As who would pray good for the world, but know
Their benediction empty as they bless.

They say that the Dead die not, but remain
  Near to the rich heirs of their grief and mirth.
    I think they ride the calm mid-heaven, as these,
In wise majestic melancholy train,
  And watch the moon, and the still-raging seas,
    And men, coming and going on the earth.

(Suggested by some of the Proceedings of the Society for
Psychical Research)

Not with vain tears, when we're beyond the sun,
    We'll beat on the substantial doors, nor tread
    Those dusty high-roads of the aimless dead
Plaintive for Earth; but rather turn and run
Down some close-covered by-way of the air,
    Some low sweet alley between wind and wind,
    Stoop under faint gleams, thread the shadows, find
Some whispering ghost-forgotten nook, and there

Spend in pure converse our eternal day;
    Think each in each immediately wise;
Learn all we lacked before; hear, know, and say
    What this tumultuous body now denies;
And feel, who have laid our groping hands away;
    And see, no longer blinded by our eyes.

Waikiki

Warm perfumes like a breath from vine and tree
    Drift down the darkness. Plangent, hidden from eyes,
    Somewhere an eukaleli thrills and cries
And stabs with pain the night's brown savagery.
And dark scents whisper; and dim waves creep to me,
    Gleam like a woman's hair, stretch out, and rise;
    And new stars burn into the ancient skies,
Over the murmurous soft Hawaian sea.

And I recall, lose, grasp, forget again,
    And still remember, a tale I have heard, or known—
An empty tale, of idleness and pain,
    Of two that loved—or did not love—and one
Whose perplexed heart did evil, foolishly,
A long while since, and by some other sea.

RUPERT BROOKE
The Dead I

Blow out, you bugles, over the rich Dead!
　　There's none of these so lonely and poor of old,
　　But, dying, has made us rarer gifts than gold.
These laid the world away; poured out the red
Sweet wine of youth; gave up the years to be
　　Of work and joy, and that unhoped serene,
　　That men call age; and those who would have been,
Their sons, they gave, their immortality.

Blow, bugles, blow! They brought us, for our dearth,
　　Holiness, lacked so long, and Love, and Pain.
Honour has come back, as a king, to earth,
And paid his subjects with a royal wage;
　　And Nobleness walks in our ways again;
And we have come into our heritage.

WILFRED OWEN
Anthem for Doomed Youth

What passing-bells for these who die as cattle?
　　Only the monstrous anger of the guns.
Only the stuttering rifles' rapid rattle
　　Can patter out their hasty orisons.
No mockeries for them; no prayers or bells,
　　Nor any voice of mourning save the choirs,—
The shrill, demented choirs of wailing shells;
　　And bugles calling for them from sad shires.

What candles may be held to speed them all?
　　Not in the hands of boys, but in their eyes
　　Shall shine the holy glimmer of good-byes.
The pallor of girls' brows shall be their pall;
　　Their flowers the tenderness of silent minds,
　　And each slow dusk a drawing-down of blinds.

EDMUND BLUNDEN

The Poor Man's Pig

Already fallen plum-bloom stars the green
   And apple-boughs as knarred as old toads' backs
Wear their small roses ere a rose is seen;
   The building thrush watches old Job who stacks
The bright-peeled osiers on the sunny fence;
   The pent sow grunts to hear him stumping by,
And tries to push the bolt and scamper thence,
   But her ringed snout still keeps her to the sty.

Then out he lets her run; away she snorts
   In bundling gallop for the cottage door,
With hungry hubbub begging crusts and orts,
   Then like a whirlwind bumping round once more;
Nuzzling the dog, making the pullets run,
   And sulky as a child when her play's done.

ROY CAMPBELL

The Zebras

From the dark woods that breathe of fallen showers,
Harnessed with level rays in golden reins,
The zebras draw the dawn across the plains
Wading knee-deep among the scarlet flowers.
The sunlight, zithering their flanks with fire,
Flashes between the shadows as they pass
Barred with electric tremors through the grass
Like wind along the gold strings of a lyre.

Into the flushed air snorting rosy plumes
That smoulder round their feet in drifting fumes,
With dove-like voices call the distant fillies,
While round the herds the stallion wheels his flight,
Engine of beauty volted with delight,
To roll his mare among the trampled lilies.

ROY CAMPBELL

The Serf

His naked skin clothed in the torrid mist
That puffs in smoke around the patient hooves,
The ploughman drives, a slow somnambulist,
And through the green his crimson furrow grooves.
His heart, more deeply than he wounds the plain,
Long by the rasping share of insult torn,
Red clod, to which the war-cry once was rain
And tribal spears the fatal sheaves of corn,
Lies fallow now. But as the turf divides
I see in the slow progress of his strides
Over the toppled clods and falling flowers,
The timeless, surly patience of the serf
That moves the nearest to the naked earth
And ploughs down palaces, and thrones, and towers.

WILLIAM PLOMER

Dragon-fly Love

Plated with light I float a thousand-eyed,
On rustling wings of veiny talc to fly,
To kiss in flight the image of my pride
That skims the deep reflection of the sky,
Where finny shoals in shadowy grace repose:
Insects that perish with a tiny cry
Provide the speed with which my body goes
In scaly splendour quadruplaning by.

Giddy with hope I seize my love at noon;
On tremulous wave of fiery air we run,
Long locked in love, across the red lagoon,
Blazing delirious while we whirl as one—
Diamonds melting underneath the moon,
Planets in union going round the sun.

INDEX OF AUTHORS

INDEX OF AUTHORS

INDEX OF AUTHORS

INDEX OF FIRST LINES

INDEX OF FIRST LINES

INDEX OF FIRST LINES

INDEX OF FIRST LINES

INDEX OF FIRST LINES